THE ULTIMATE GUIDE
TO THE ART OF CLEANING

Jeff Campbell and The Clean Team, the experts who can get a house spruced up and sparkling in minutes flat, face cleaning horrors and dirt disasters daily. Their job depends on getting household items, furniture, and doodads looking like new. And they can't take hours doing it.

Once again they are ready to share their trade secrets—simple, timesaving, environmentally sound solutions to the 157 most frequently encountered cleaning problems.

It takes more than elbow grease to handle these babies! So Jeff Campbell and The Clean Team give you the lowdown and dirt on each and every one. After all, none of us can escape death, taxes . . . or household cleaning. Now you can dream the impossible dream . . . and get rid of the impossible dirt!

TALKING DIRT
WHEN SOAP AND WATER AREN'T ENOUGH

Books by Jeff Campbell
of The Clean Team

SPEED CLEANING
SPRING CLEANING
CLUTTER CONTROL

TALKING DIRT

AMERICA'S SPEED CLEANING EXPERT
ANSWERS THE 157 MOST ASKED
CLEANING QUESTIONS

Jeff Campbell
of The Clean Team

A DELL TRADE PAPERBACK

A DELL TRADE PAPERBACK

Published by
Dell Publishing
a division of
Bantam Doubleday Dell Publishing Group, Inc.
1540 Broadway
New York, New York 10036

Library of Congress Cataloging in Publication Data
Campbell, Jeff.
    Talking dirt: America's speed cleaning expert answers the 157 most asked cleaning questions / Jeff Campbell of The Clean Team.
        p.   cm.
    ISBN 0-440-50788-X
    1. House cleaning.   I. Clean Team (San Francisco, Calif.)   II. Title.
TX324.C374   1997
648—dc21   96-37633
                                                                            CIP

Printed in the United States of America

Published simultaneously in Canada

FFG

To Dan and Peggy

They deserve great happiness
and have earned great success

Acknowledgments

My thanks again to Bill Redican for his editorial collaboration throughout this book, our fourth on this subject. His writing skills and his cleaning knowledge are world class.

Illustrator Axelle Fortier has also made the subject of cleaning more palatable for the fourth time. Her sense of humor and dedication are valuable assets.

Frank Gromm III, of Gromm's Rug and Upholstery Cleaners, Montara, California, once again offered expert advice on carpet care.

Carolyn Tallent, a paintings conservator from Santa Monica, California, came to our rescue regarding a particularly difficult question on the care of paintings.

Dr. Geraldine Somers of Boston, Massachusetts, took time from her hectic schedule to offer a professional point of view on the use of disinfectants in the home.

Daniel Hershberger, veterinarian extraordinaire and partner of All Pets Hospital in San Francisco, educated me about the lifestyle of the lowly flea in terms I could understand.

Phillip Shamlian, owner (along with his sister Margaret) of San Francisco's Bay City Paints, and Wayne Foster, manager of Floors to Go in Jackson, California, shared their expertise on questions about hardwood floors.

Al Hale, owner of San Francisco's Accurate Appliances, has kept both The Clean Team's and my home's appliances in tip-top condition for over fifteen years. He was invaluable with expert advice about household appliances, their problems, and their solutions.

Clervi Marble Company's Attilio Meschi, in San Francisco, was a wealth of information about marble and granite. I look forward to talking with him again.

Julie Ann Ast, owner of Tile Import Store in Jackson, California, shared her expertise on tile floors and, even more important, grout.

At The Clean Team Catalog in Boca Raton, Florida, Peggy Nordeen and Jeff Lillie critiqued early drafts of this book mercilessly—and made it better. Just as important, thanks to all the staff there—particularly those in customer service, who helped gather together the all-important questions!

My friend Jesus Omila, Jr., protected us against excess crankiness by keeping Bill, Axelle, and me well fed and downright comfortable during very long working weekends.

Linda Brown suggested the title. I started a speech to a group of bed-and-breakfast owners by saying, "We're here to talk dirt!" She said: "That's it! That's the title for your new book." We shortened it a bit, but she was right.

Thanks. Linda and her husband, Louis, own The Chaska House in Waxahachie, Texas.

Once again, thanks to Mike Curry, Phil Nordeng, and my other partners and colleagues at The Clean Team Cleaning Company for sharing their expertise and friendship.

And Rudy! What would I—or anyone at The Clean Team—do without Rudy? Rudy Dinkel, that is. Thanks so much.

If you give up ever cleaning the house at all, it doesn't seem to get any dirtier after the first six months. The trick is to not lose your nerve.

—**Quentin Crisp**

Rest is not idleness, and to lie sometimes on the grass under the trees on a summer's day, listening to the murmur of the water, or watching the clouds float across the blue sky, is by no means a waste of time.

—**Sir John Lubbock**

Contents

1 Where These Questions Came From   1

2 Kitchens   10

3 Bathrooms   34

4 Other Rooms   60

5 Floors   103

6 Carpets   128

7 Windows   147

8 Products   159

Glossary   179

Appendix:
How to Order Tools, Equipment, and Supplies   206

Index   208

Chapter 1

WHERE THESE QUESTIONS CAME FROM

Recently my neighbors introduced me to a friend who promptly asked me a question about housecleaning. People ask me such questions fairly often. But I was just starting this book, so I was particularly interested in her question, and I wanted to articulate an especially brilliant reply.

She asked me how to clean light fixtures that were similar to ones I have in my kitchen. The fixtures are heavy, awkward, and made of clear glass. Airborne kitchen grease settles on them, so they look dirty much of the time.

I began to tell her how to wash such fixtures by hand in the sink, the big secret being to use a *toothbrush* to clean the grooves that trap greasy dirt. She explained, "No, no, no. I couldn't do that!" So I cleverly offered an alternative: "Put them in the dishwasher." Her reply: "No, no. You don't understand. I don't do things like that." It was as if I were proposing an exotic form of mating ritual.

So I learned, as I started this project, that people often ask cleaning questions in a style that doesn't actually lead to their doing anything. For years I had been answering cleaning questions and assuming that people were following my advice, not just ruminating over it. So this new insight was somewhat discouraging.

Then there's the case of my friend who asked me how to get rid of *hard-water spots* in his shower. I told him to use a *squeegee*, but he interrupted and told me that he knew about squeegees and he "couldn't bear the thought" of using one. So I started to tell him about how to remove the spots with a *tile brush*, *Tile Juice*, and a *white pad*. He knew all about these too, and he didn't like this solution any better.

And so I next concluded that people sometimes ask cleaning questions as a form of wishful thinking: they already feel they know the answer, but they don't like it, and they are casting about for a more palatable one. Hmm.

Other folks appear to ask housecleaning questions to demonstrate their interest and to feel that they are really doing something positive about their housecleaning problems. They also seem to neglect to make actual plans to act on the answer, however. It's akin to buying a wax stripper and then storing it under the kitchen sink for the rest of your natural life. It's as if the activity of inquiring or buying would itself strip the wax off the floor.

If one is to benefit from a housecleaning question, one must accept, nay, even embrace, the fact that the answer inevitably should lead to an activity, usually one of a housecleaning nature, although it's always possible that the answer could be to move, to sell the house, or to run for the hills. But the answer should also lessen stress when it's time to do the cleaning. It should enable you to feel better about your ability to keep the home front civilized, comfortable, and relatively presentable. Feelings of guilt and frustration should be replaced with feelings of accomplishment.

Our teachers told us that the only stupid question is the one that isn't asked. And I've been asked thousands and thousands of cleaning questions since The Clean Team (my cleaning company) first started. Not long ago an article about The Clean Team appeared in a magazine devoted to country life. At the end of the article people were invited to call with their cleaning questions. And they sure did—in droves. I discovered that cleaning problems that *don't* involve pigs, cows, horses, goats (and births thereof!), flies, manure, tree sap, grease, barns, and wheat, barley, or oat chaff are much, much easier to answer than ones that do. That was a real eye-opener.

I once wrote an article to be distributed, as part of a kit, to people returning to their homes after a flood. This was a case where the correct answer to a cleaning question was to move out of the home! Questions about cleaning after a fire also tend to yield answers that are very difficult to implement.

So. Those of you who are having a hard time revving yourself up for action—even after you have the answer to your cleaning question—remember there are cleaning problems vastly more difficult than your own. I know that's just like my mother telling me to eat my food because people were starving abroad, but, hey, it worked.

If you are a first-time reader, you may be asking yourself, Who the heck is The Clean Team? Well, it's San Francisco's busiest housecleaning service. We clean San Francisco homes at the rate of about eighteen thousand times a year. I founded the company in 1979, and I've written three other books about the housecleaning skills we've learned the hard way in almost twenty years.

The first thing we learned was that if we were going to earn a living, we had to complete just about every one of the eighteen thousand cleanings efficiently. This means learning how to get the cleaning over with *fast*. Whether money is involved or not, who doesn't want to get their cleaning over with more quickly?

Those cleaning trade secrets became our first book, *Speed Cleaning*. That book has become a cleaning bible to many, and a decade later it is still a perennial steady seller. *Speed Cleaning* shows you how to finish weekly or every-other-week cleaning in minutes instead of hours. It was followed by *Spring Cleaning*, which teaches you how to complete occasional cleaning tasks with skill and efficiency. *Clutter Control*, the third book, addresses the subject of household organization: how to keep the house from being overwhelmed by paper, products, and other modern detritus, how to locate things in the house on purpose instead of by accident, and how to keep the household civilized enough to tackle the weekly cleaning chores.

Part of cleaning well involves choosing the right cleaning products and tools. Starting with *Speed Cleaning*, we have listed the products that The Clean Team has found to be the best and the fastest—after testing them in thousands of homes. Since *Speed Cleaning* was published, we've been receiving tens of thousands of letters a year requesting information about where to get these products. The Clean Team Catalog Company was

formed to help make available safe, fast, and professional products for the homes of interested nonprofessional cleaners: legions of busy, harried professional working people who want to get the housecleaning over with and move on to the more interesting things life has to offer.

Don't be alarmed. We're not going to try to sell you cleaning supplies or even suggest that you might be happier if you changed the brands you use. As pleased as we are with what we've learned about cleaning products, that wouldn't be fair. The book is about solving cleaning problems for *you*. But in the interest of simplicity, when we refer to a cleaning product, we will specify the name of the product The Clean Team prefers. For example, for a heavy-duty liquid cleaner like Fantastik, Formula 409, or Simple Green, we'll refer to *Red Juice*. For a glass cleaner like Windex or Glass Plus, we'll refer to *Blue Juice*. Any product printed in *italics* is further explained in the glossary. Unless otherwise indicated, when we list consumer products that we don't use on a daily basis, we are just giving examples. We are not expressing an opinion one way or the other as to their merits or demerits because of the wide range of surfaces, dirt, and conditions of exposure in households. (Besides, their legal department is bigger than our legal department.)

The Clean Team tests cleaning products regularly. These days manufacturers even send us new products to test. We look at more than just how they clean. First, is the product being tested personally safe? We insist that the products we use day after day be user friendly because we're exposed to them far longer than the average consumer. We look for products that are nontoxic, use as little dye as possible, don't smell awful, don't make it hard to breathe, and don't burn or otherwise irritate our skin or eyes. No matter how effective a product is, if it causes grief to the person who's using it, it isn't going to pass our test. In addition, we select products that do an excellent job at whatever it is they are supposed to do, and do it quickly. Next, they must not degrade the environment. Finally, if we find two or more cleaners to be equally safe, equally effective, and equally fast, then we consider cost. If a product saves time because it outperforms another product, even if it costs more initially, the additional expense is usually slight—especially over the life of the product—and negligible compared with the leisure time added to your life. (If you would like to know more about any of The Clean Team products, see the Appendix, "How to Order Tools, Equipment, and Supplies." Catalogs are free.)

Also, we rely on products that everyone can purchase. We don't experiment by mixing chemicals, and we don't advise you to start mixing them either. Some people mix chemicals in the belief that they are making a cleaner that is safer for the environment, cheaper, or more effective. These goals usually aren't accomplished, and in the meantime scads of precious leisure time can be wasted. Products manufactured by reputable companies with advanced-degree chemists and million-dollar labs routinely manage to produce something more effective than what you make in your kitchen sink. In addition, household chemistry can be downright dangerous. The most common hazard comes from mixing chlorine *bleach* with *ammonia*. Every year a few people in the United States die because they mixed the two. (Ammonia releases the toxic gas from the bleach.)

But don't be dismayed if you enjoy making your own cleaning products. As long as you enjoy doing so, go right ahead, and use them in good health. In any event the answers we present in this book will work with your products also. That's because we discuss processes as well as products. If you follow the process, despite using different cleaning products, you'll still get the job done.

When answering questions, we try to give the single best answer. We avoid the easy answer: "Try this, and if it doesn't work, try that, and then the other." But sometimes a single answer doesn't work. For example, one surface may require a different cleaning process from another, and the only way to find out in that particular case is to try various solutions.

We still get questions every day. We call upon nearly twenty years of cleaning experience, along with the valuable information we learn from our readers, friends, and suppliers, to help people solve cleaning problems. We've learned a lot about what people want to know about housecleaning. Your most frequently asked questions are answered in this book. The other three books were written from our point of view as professional housecleaners. This book gives you a chance to get answers on what's bothering you. You can fine-tune your housecleaning to save even more time and effort—all so you can reclaim more of your precious free time.

If by chance we didn't answer the one question that's been driving you crazy, please give us a call, and we'll do our best: 1-800-717-CLEAN.

Chapter 2

KITCHENS

1. Wood Cabinets

There are beautiful wood cabinets on three walls of my kitchen. I've had them for six or seven years, and I know I should be doing something for them. However, I've done nothing. They're getting stickier and greasier, so please tell me what to do.

It sounds as if the time to take action has arrived. Here's what to do. Use a product like *Furniture Feeder*.* It's carnauba wax suspended in a solvent solution. The solvent removes the grease, fingerprints, splattered mustard and chocolate, long-dried spritzes of Pepsi, and so forth. The carnauba wax protects, reinvigorates, and adds new shine to the underlying coating on the cabinets.

It's a big job, however. Seven-year-old kitchen grease does not give up without a fight. Apply Furniture Feeder to the cabinets by pouring some

* Remember, anytime you see a word in italics, you will find an entry in the glossary.

onto an old *cleaning cloth*. Starting at the top and in one corner of the kitchen, wipe the cabinets in small areas at a time. Dip a *toothbrush* into Furniture Feeder to clean corners, hard-to-get-at areas, or hard-to-remove spots. Add generous amounts of Furniture Feeder to your cloth regularly. Wipe each area clean, dry, and shiny with a separate cleaning cloth, or use a *polishing cloth* to achieve a bit more shine. This treatment with Furniture Feeder is a spring cleaning chore that comes up only once a year or so. During weekly cleaning trips around the kitchen, spot-clean the cabinets with *Red Juice*.

As you clean the cabinets, you will undoubtedly notice that the hinges are also filthy. That is another case where a simple toothbrush tool can quickly scrub away dirt, grime, and other gunk from the nooks, crannies, and crevices that make up a decorative cabinet hinge. Go ahead and clean all the hinges before you continue with the cabinets themselves. Just grab some Red Juice and spray, agitate with the toothbrush, and wipe with a cleaning cloth. If necessary, because of the design of the cabinet or hinge, open the cabinet door, and repeat from the inside. It's quick and nearly painless. You've probably forgotten how nice the cabinets looked when they were new.

2. Butcher Block

I have a butcher block that I use to protect the tile counter and to prepare food on. There's nothing wrong with it as far as I know, but I caught the last bit of a talk show and someone was talking about how dangerous such blocks were. You know, salmonella and other scary bacteria. What did I miss? What should I do to keep it clean?

Probably not much more than what you're doing now. But here's the scoop. If you cut poultry on your butcher block (or plastic cutting board or other surface) and then prepare uncooked food on the same surface, you could transfer salmonella from the poultry to the other food. The salmonella on the poultry will be destroyed by proper cooking, but you and your family could be made seriously ill by the salmonella on the uncooked food.

Clean the butcher block between uses with warm, soapy water. I use a plastic scrub pad (S.O.S. Tuffy dishwashing pad) to scrub the surface. Then rinse the block with hot water, and wipe it dry. If the block is too big to move, wipe the suds off with a couple of paper towels, and then wipe dry with a final paper towel. Allow to air-dry thoroughly. You should be washing the knife (and your hands) as well. If you can remember to do it, use one side of the block for fruits and veggies and the other side for meats. While we're at it, wash your dish towels regularly. Wash and rinse sponges well, and allow them to air-dry. Pop sponges in the dishwasher occasionally, and throw them away once they start looking funky. Don't try to rehabilitate ones that smell bad: toss them.

Occasionally treat the butcher block with a coat of walnut oil. Wash it well, as described above, and allow it to dry several hours or overnight. Pour walnut oil onto the butcher block and spread it around with a paper towel. Use a bit more than is necessary and allow the oil to remain on the surface for a few minutes. Then wipe away the excess with several paper towels. It will look like new again for a few months.

3. White Countertop Stains

When I got married, I brought my coffee habit to my husband's almost new house. Periodically the coffee would spill and stain the kitchen's off-white counter. Because I'm an infection control nurse, I cleaned it up with bleach. For a long time that worked. Now it's stained—and it won't clean up! I should also add that three teenagers tend to spill the orange juice in the same area. Needless to say, my new husband has observed that the stains weren't there until I came.

I was interested in your sentence "Periodically the coffee would spill. . . ." Not "I spilled the coffee," eh? Sort of like "It broke" instead of "I broke it." Isn't language wonderful?

What has probably happened is that repeated applications of *bleach* have damaged the countertop. Bleach can eat at the surface in a way that you may not even be able to see, but it's making the surface rougher and rougher. Rough surfaces have millions of tiny crevices and grooves that trap stain makers, such as coffee and orange juice, making them almost impossible to remove.

Unfortunately, the ultimate solution is to replace the countertop. But you

can still solve the immediate problem by protecting it better. First, clean it one more time. Use a *white pad* or #0000 steel wool along with *Red Juice* and even some more chlorine *bleach solution* or hydrogen peroxide. It can be done; it's just getting harder and harder to do it. Then protect the countertop from further spills. Put a cutting board—either wood or plastic—or a place mat over the area where you and the kids pour your juice and coffee. Wipe up spills before they can drip off the board onto the countertop.

4.   Granite Stain

My kitchen work station has a granite surface of many different shades of pink and black. It's absolutely gorgeous, and I just love it. So I was heartbroken to find that a wet teabag has left a small but very noticeable stain on it. What can I do to save this beautiful stone?

To research your question, I went to San Francisco's preeminent stone dealer, Clervi Marble Co. It was my pleasure to meet Attilio Meschi, a man who has worked with granite, marble, and other types of natural stone for forty years. He travels to Italy regularly to oversee his supply of raw materials, and he was a wealth of information. I wanted to apply for his job, but that's another story. . . .

First try to remove the stain with 12 percent hydrogen peroxide and a few drops of ammonia. (Hydrogen peroxide for bleaching hair is 12 percent; for first aid it's only 3 percent.) If that doesn't do it, Mr. Meschi recommends a poultice: a cleaner or chemical mixed with an absorbent material and then applied to the stain. An organic stain should respond to a poultice of hydrogen peroxide and Bon Ami. You may substitute talc, white molding plaster, powdered chalk, whiting, or fuller's earth for Bon Ami. (Mr. Meschi actually uses 32 percent hydrogen peroxide and painter's whiting, which may make the work go a bit faster but are more difficult to find.) Mix the two ingredients to the consistency of cake frosting, and use a plastic scraper or spatula to apply it $1/4$ to $1/2$ inch thick over the stain. Cover the poultice with plastic sheeting or plastic food wrap and tape the edges to the granite. (If you use a tape like blue Scotch masking tape that doesn't leave any residue, you won't have that problem to deal with later.) Allow it all to remain for twenty-four hours. Then remove the tape and plastic and allow the poultice to dry for another twenty-four hours. Wipe off the poultice, clean the area with water, dry with a cleaning cloth, and inspect the stain. If it disappeared, great. If the stain is lighter, repeat the process. If it's not improved after three tries, give up or call a professional.

A poultice can also be made using cotton balls or gauze pads. For small stains such as yours, that might be easier. Put either over the stain, wet with the hydrogen peroxide (but not to the point of dripping). Then cover and tape as above. You can also substitute acetone for hydrogen peroxide. Actually, if the granite is quite dark, it would be safer to try the acetone first because of the very slim possibility of a bleaching effect from the hydrogen peroxide. As usual, it's also smart to pretest.

For oil stains, the poultice can be made with: (a) baking soda and water, (b) poultice powder (e.g., Bon Ami) plus mineral spirits, or (c) cotton balls or gauze plus mineral spirits. **Note:** granite is far more resistant to stains and acids than is marble. (See Questions 41 and 62.) But as you are only too well aware, "resistant" doesn't mean that it won't stain at all. To guard against stains, most natural stone surfaces should be sealed and perhaps also waxed. Check with your installer or other professional for a recommendation about products for your particular stone.

5. Stained Porcelain Sinks

I have a white porcelain sink. I have not been happy with the way it looks lately. It seems to stain easily from coffee, et cetera, and my stainless steel pans make black marks on it. I have used a soft-scrub bleach product, but that still does not get up the black marks. I have also used Zud and a nylon Scotch-Brite pad. They worked, but now the surface of the sink seems rough.

Your question reminds me of the child who complained about how much it hurt when he hit his finger with a hammer. The advice from his father: "Quit hitting it, then." Since coffee stains it, and pots and pans make black marks, pour leftover coffee directly into the drain, and use a protective pad or position a sponge to keep the pans from direct contact with the porcelain. I'm not just being flip; it makes sense to provide this sort of protection to reduce the number of stains and black marks you produce.

You're right in noticing that the sink surface is less smooth. Aggressive cleaning with harsh products damages the porcelain over time. Intensive, lengthy rubbing of a surface with practically any cleaning product (harsh or not) can damage the surface. Green pads, metal cleaning pads, or steel wool can be murder on surfaces. In most cases the damage consists of small scratches in the surface in which all manner of stains get trapped.

Liquid or paste finishes like *Bathroom Barrier* are available for sinks (also tubs, shower walls, shower doors, fiberglass and acrylic spas, et cetera). Such products provide a protective barrier. The dirt is easier to remove from the smooth surface of the protectant than from the rougher surface of the porcelain itself. As you might guess, protectants can also add a bit of shine to the surface. They are designed to be applied only occasionally—something like car wax. Although they save cleaning time, it will obviously take time to apply them. You'll have to decide if you're willing to put in a bit of extra effort to get nicer-looking and nicer-feeling surfaces. **Note:** New sinks, tubs, tiles, et cetera, are free of scratches and therefore far easier to clean. In fact plain *Red Juice* or other liquid cleaner is all you need for new fixtures. Don't use powdered cleanser or even "soft" cleansers on a new sink by habit. Wait until you actually need them.

6. Rusty Stainless Sink

The rust on my stainless steel sink is becoming intolerable. I thought stainless didn't rust. How can I get rid of it?

On the basis of the available information, we can't be sure if the rust is coming from the sink itself or from metal things attached to it (like the faucet or drain ring). But the sink itself may be rusty. Stainless steel is still mainly iron, with up to 30 percent chromium. Even stainless steel deteriorates over time. It just takes longer than other steels.

Whatever the source, powdered cleanser and a *white pad* will remove most rust spots. Use a *toothbrush* on areas you can't reach with the white pad. If the white pad doesn't work well, try #0000 steel wool. The rust stains or rust in porcelain sinks, tubs, et cetera, can also be removed with a special rust-neutralizing product (e.g., *Rust Remover*, Bar Keepers Friend, Zud) that contains oxalic acid. Oxalic acid is the main weapon against rust problems of all sorts. (See Question 45.)

7. Stainless Steel Stove Hood

I have a stove with a stainless steel hood. I can't seem to remove splattered grease from this area. What should I do?

Cooked-on grease calls for a grease cutter (*Red Juice*) and a *white pad* or #0000 steel wool. Since the hood is stainless steel, we advise using a white pad because even #0000 steel wool can scratch the finish of stainless steel. Scrub with a *toothbrush* as needed in corners. Resort to a heavy *degreaser* such as our Monster Green, if the grease is very old and is impossible to remove otherwise.

Keep this area from becoming a problem so quickly by keeping the filter clean (see Question 8) and by wiping the hood inside and out when you do your weekly cleaning. **Note:** We didn't refer you to a specialized stainless steel cleaner because one isn't necessary. However, stainless steel cleaners add a sheen that many find appealing.

8. Exhaust Filters

The aluminum filter in the hood of my stove has *never* been cleaned as far as I know. It's a greasy mess. I doubt if it even works anymore because it's so encrusted with grease. Is there hope for my pathetic little filter?

The situation may be hopeless, but you can always have hope. In this case the answer is easy. Pop the filter in the dishwasher. You may have to run it through a couple of times, but it will eventually come clean. It pays to keep the filter clean because when it is and the fan is on, it will pull in a lot of grease that would otherwise accumulate on nearby surfaces. And those surfaces can't simply be "popped" into the dishwasher. **Note:** You'd be surprised how cheap a replacement filter is.

9.   Greasy Backsplashes

The tile backsplashes behind the kitchen counters have a serious buildup of grease or something of similar ilk. We have scrubbed with soap and water using the green sponge I use on pots and pans, but our efforts do not seem to be doing any good. Any suggestions?

Soap or detergent alone isn't strong enough for this kind of grease buildup, so you need *Red Juice* because it's a more powerful grease cutter. (You may find that a moderate clear *ammonia solution* works better than Red Juice on some types of grease.) Also, just as it helps to soak pots and pans that have baked-on grease, it helps to soak a heavy buildup of grease on tiles. To do this, spray the tiles with Red Juice; then go back and respray them a few minutes later. Keep the grease wet with Red Juice for fifteen minutes or more before you start scrubbing. (Strategically position a few *cleaning cloths* to catch the runoff.) If the grease is especially thick, first remove most of it with a *scraper*; a plastic one is safe on all hard surfaces. Then use a *stiff-bristled brush* because bristles cut through the grease better than sponges or even *white pads*. They also clean the grout lines along with the tile. Continue wetting with Red Juice as you work.

If the tiles are plastic or have been painted, the grease may have chemically interacted with the surface. If so, the paint or plastic will be permanently stained, and the grease can't be removed without damaging the tiles or removing the paint.

10. Greasy Bricks

I've managed to splatter grease on a red-brick wall, and it's resisting all efforts to clean it. Suggestions, anyone?

If there's a stove in front of the wall, first move it away if you can do so safely. (Careful with the gas line and fixtures.) Trying to clean a wall while constantly reaching over a stove is more trouble than finding someone to help you move the stove to begin with. Next, liberally spray with *Red Juice* (or a moderate clear *ammonia solution*) and use a *stiff-bristled brush* to agitate the greasy area. Sop up the mess with *cleaning cloths* or paper towels. Try wrapping the brush with a cleaning cloth to make it easier to remove dirty cleaning solution from the brick's irregular surfaces. Because brick is so porous, you'll probably have to repeat this process several times. The bricks may never get satisfactorily clean. You may have to paint them or otherwise cover them with a backsplash of some sort. A backsplash is a good idea in any event. It's a whole lot easier to clean than bricks.

Some types of old brick could be soft enough to be damaged by vigorous brushing and cleaning. Test, and if this is the case, just dust, wipe, ignore, or move.

11. "Miracle" Mops

What do you think of those exotic mops that are sold on TV every hour of the day and night?

I hope you don't feel bad if you've bought one, but I think they're a waste of money. I suspect that not one of them has been offered because it rep-

FAMOUS MOVIE STAR SAYS

"I LOST 25 POUNDS, THANKS TO MY MARVELOUS, NEW, *Miracle Mop!*"
Famous Movie Star

resents a legitimate advance in the evolution of the mop, but rather because some marketing-driven company is out to make a buck—or a million of them—if they can talk us into buying one. A European-style *flat mop* with a terry cloth cover is so much better. The American version we use is quite similar. It's genuinely faster, it doesn't recycle dirty water back to the floor, and it reaches under appliances and into corners. Because its terry cloth covers are washable, it's like a new mop each time you use it.

12. "Self-Cleaning" Ovens

How do you clean self-cleaning ovens?

This really is a good question, but I can't help thinking of questions like "What time is midnight Mass?" or "Who's buried in Grant's tomb?" Self-cleaning or no, ovens always seem to be in some state of dirtiness. And some of us are nervous about the high heat and odor created by self-cleaning ovens—or the power bill that follows—and prefer not to use the self-cleaning cycle. In any event you must follow the manufacturer's directions to the letter. Don't try to clean them with oven cleaners like Easy-Off, Dow, Mr. Muscle, and so forth. For spots the automatic cleaning cycle misses (such as the edges of the door), use *Red Juice* and a *white pad* or green pad. To clean a spattered oven window quickly, use Red Juice and a razor in a holder. Be protective of the oven once it's clean. Use aluminum foil if there's any chance a dish will overflow during baking. Wipe up little spills ASAP. Clean baked-on blackened spots without cleaning the whole oven by spraying with Red Juice and coaxing them off with a *pumice stick*.

13.   Stove Tops

How do I clean the greasy electric burners on my stove?

You don't. You clean around them and under them, but not the burners themselves. If you have spilled something thick and sticky, first let everything cool, then clean the stove top with *Red Juice*, gently wipe the burner, clean under the burner where you may need a white or green pad or even #0000 steel wool (see Question 14), and finally turn it on to the highest temperature to burn off whatever remains. Have the exhaust fan on or the windows open to avoid setting off a smoke detector.

14. Drip Trays Under Burners

The trays under my stove's burners are nasty. Nothing gets them clean; even your dishwasher idea didn't make much improvement. Should I give up and throw them away?

Yes! That's exactly what you should do. Replace these trays every few years when they don't come clean any longer or whenever they start to drive you crazy. As with aluminum filters for stove-top exhaust fans, you'll be surprised how inexpensive replacements are.

15. Glass Stove Tops

I have a glass stove top, and I like it, but I have two problems with it. One is that it shows streaks after cleaning, and two is that difficult stains are sometimes left on it after cooking.

There are streaks on porcelain stove tops also; it's just that they don't show up the way they do on glass. The streaks are from two sources. The first is that you're probably cleaning the stove top with a sponge and soapy water or with *Red Juice* or another general cleaner. Any of these products can leave a visible streak on glass. After first using one of these products to clean, respray the stove top with *Blue Juice* or another glass cleaner, and wipe it dry with a *cleaning cloth*. The second reason it may be streaking is that you may be cleaning it while it's still warm. In that case the heat is evaporating the cleaner faster than you can wipe it off, and the result is streaks. Let it cool thoroughly first.

The stains on the stove top after cooking are probably caused by the pans you're cooking with. Wash the outside bottoms of your pots and pans well enough so they can't transfer stains when you put them on the stove top or when you move them from one spot to another.

16. Stinky Dishwashers

My dishwasher has bad breath. How do I clean it and get the smell out?

There's something fishy here. Your dishwasher should smell like the detergent used in it. I checked for advice with Al Hale, owner of Accurate Appliances in San Francisco, who has been keeping our appliances running for the last fifteen years or so. He said the most common reason for an odor is an improperly installed garbage disposal! The disposal water line may allow food from the disposal to be thrown into the dishwasher line. If you've recently installed a disposal, that could be the culprit. Three other possibilities are: (1) The rubber door gasket that forms the lower seal has started to disintegrate and is creating its own odor; (2) the heating element is burned out and gives off an odor when it cycles on and off; (3) gunk has accumulated in the area between the lower front of the dishwasher and the door. This last possibility has a cleaning solution: Clean that area carefully with a *toothbrush* and *Red Juice*. Call in a professional—like Al—for the other possibilities.

After you've solved the problem, run the dishwasher with a quarter cup of white *vinegar* to help remove any lingering odors. Start the dishwasher empty of dishes or soap. When it fills with water the first time, open the door, add the vinegar, and let the cycle complete itself.

17. Dishwasher Stains

Our eighteen-year-old dishwasher looks disgusting inside. We use well water containing minerals that stain everything after repeated use. I used Zud to help eradicate the rust coating from the walls of the washer. The interior is a speckled enamel coating. Do you have any suggestions for eliminating or at least reducing the yucky-looking stuff from the interior?

Hard-water spots can be removed by running *vinegar* through your dishwasher's cycle. As a mild acid it will help dissolve these deposits. Start the dishwasher empty, and add white vinegar after it fills with water for the first cycle. Add as much as you can without causing an overflow—up to two or three cups. Vinegar is a weak cleaner, so you may have to repeat this process.

Hard-water deposits generally don't harm the interior of the dishwasher permanently. But if the water has an extremely high mineral content, stains will start to appear on glassware and dishes and can damage the dishwasher pump. Consider installing a water softener. If you're not using liquid rinse agents already, I suggest you do so. (See Question 20.) The humane thing to do might be to give your venerable dishwasher a well-deserved rest and start over with a new one. **Note:** When doing your regular kitchen cleaning, remember to open the dishwasher as you go by and clean the interior edges of the door. This area isn't cleaned by the action of the dishwasher, and it gets rather disgusting if ignored. Use *Red Juice*, a *toothbrush*, and a *cleaning cloth*.

18.   Sticker Residue

How do I get stickers off the front of my refrigerator? I want to sell it, but the remnants of two (both now defunct!) Chinese restaurants' stick-on advertisements seem rather permanent.

I know what you mean. Pasting the stickers seemed like such a good idea at the time. The removal process starts by getting a fingernail or plastic spatula under an edge of the stickers so you can pull off the top layer and expose the glue underneath. Then use a *solvent*, such as *De-Zov-All* or lighter fluid. Apply with a paper towel, and use another one to rub the glue off. (See Question 36.)

19.   Hard-Water Deposits on Glass Shelves

I have a pop-out-window greenhouse with three glass shelves in my kitchen where I grow orchids. I've rearranged the pots, and now terrible mineral stains are visible. They were caused by water that seeped under the planter and was allowed to dry—over and over again.

Use *Tile Juice*. Squirt some on the glass, allow it to sit for a few minutes, and scrub with a *white pad*. Be careful. The glass can break quite easily. If the buildup is particularly thick, first spray with *Red Juice* or even water to get it wet, and then use a single-edge razor in a holder to scrape most of the *hard-water spot* off. It's safer and faster to remove the shelf to do this. Put the shelf on a flat surface so it will be safely supported when you scrape with the razor. After you've removed most of the buildup with the razor, apply Tile Juice as above. For general cleaning, and if they fit, put the glass shelves into the dishwasher. **Note:** Don't use terra-cotta saucers directly on the glass because they aren't waterproof and moisture seeps through. Even though water hasn't overflowed, a stain can be forming. Use a glass or plastic saucer instead of, or under, the terra-cotta saucer.

20.   Hard-Water Deposits on Dishes

I think I have hard-water spots on my dishes. Is that possible?

Sure is, and it's happened to me too. The person I bought a set of black dishes from, and to whom I subsequently griped about the dramatic visibility of *hard-water spots,* gave me the answer to this question. At the grocery store, in the same area as dishwasher soap, is a product known as a liquid rinse agent. Add it to the dishwasher's dispenser for automatic rinse agents. My dishwasher has such a dispenser—right next to where I add the detergent. *Voilà!* No more hard-water spots. I've also learned that #0000 steel wool will quickly remove hard-water spots from drinking glasses.

21. Salt and Pepper Shakers

I know it sounds stupid, but how do you clean salt and pepper shakers? The ones I leave out on the stove look really disgusting. Wiping them with a wet sponge as I clean after cooking doesn't do a thing.

That's not a stupid question at all. Ever notice how much time restaurant staffs spend cleaning salt and pepper shakers? Sitting there on the stove at home, they're collecting grease, grime, and splatters plus enough heat to harden them into a film that's nasty to get off. However, *Red Juice* and a *white pad* will clean them nicely and with minimum effort. Then clean the holes with a toothpick.

22. Can Openers

How do you clean a can opener? Mine is so disgusting, I might just have to throw it away and start over again.

Don't toss your can opener in the can just yet. If it's a hand-operated one, put the whole thing in the dishwasher. (First give it a quick scrubbing with a *toothbrush* and a shot of *Red Juice*.) If it's electric, slide the cutting mechanism away from the body of the opening, and put only that part in the dishwasher. The body can easily be cleaned with Red Juice, a *cleaning cloth*, and probably a toothbrush. *Any* small appliance, with difficult-to-get-to knobs, buttons, corners, and molded parts is an ideal place for a toothbrush to come to the rescue. Naturally, do unplug small appliances before you start bathing them in Red Juice or anything else.

Chapter 3

BATHROOMS

23. Shower and Counter Grout

How should I clean grout? Both the shower and countertops have nasty-looking grout. Help!

As you've discovered, grout is one of the most difficult surfaces to clean. It is both rough and porous at the same time. Rough surfaces are more difficult to clean than smooth ones, and dirt sinks into porous areas—out of reach of your cleaning efforts. Moreover, grout lines themselves are recessed, so most cleaning tools glide right over them. Some cleaning tools actually make the grout dirtier by pushing dirt from nearby surfaces into the grout. This is especially true when you clean a floor. (See Question 24.)

A *brush*, along with the appropriate cleaner (*Tile Juice* in showers and *Red Juice* on counters), is the best way to get at the grout surface and dig out embedded dirt. Use a *tile brush* in a shower and, depending on the area to be cleaned, a *toothbrush* or a handheld *stiff-bristled brush* on a counter. When cleaning vertical surfaces such as shower walls, you can really put some muscle behind a brush, but grout on horizontal surfaces like countertops can be damaged by hard scrubbing. Grease, oil, coffee, or chocolate spilled on a counter isn't moved along by gravity to a drain. Instead the grout becomes impregnated. Many household products (e.g., grease) weaken grout to the point that heavy scrubbing with a stiff-bristled brush will actually remove grout rather than clean it!

When cleaning countertop grout for the first time, go gently until you learn how strong or weak the grout actually is. If the grout has been soaked with various stains and has not been maintained well for a long period of time, you may not be able to get it clean again. Clean what you can without further damaging the grout. Let the cleaner sit on the grout a bit longer and gently use a toothbrush or other brush. Ultimately regrouting might be the best solution.

Protect new tile-and-grout countertops by being vigilant. Wipe up spills of all types—even plain tap water—promptly. **Note:** A *grout sealer* can save lots of time by reducing the porosity of the grout. Apply it to new grout, and then reapply it every six months or so. On old grout or when reapplying sealer, first clean the grout as well as you can. Allow the grout to dry, and then apply the sealer.

24.   Floor Grout

How can I get the grout in my ceramic tile floor white again?

Here's what to do occasionally, as a spring cleaning project. When the floor is completely dry, vacuum the grout lines well. Use the crevice attachment, if necessary, to remove all loose dirt. Now prepare a clear *ammonia solution*. About a cup of ammonia per gallon of water should do, but feel free to add more ammonia if necessary. Use a floor *brush* to apply the ammonia solution. Dip the brush into the solution, position a row of bristles directly in a grout line, and scrub away. Use the ammonia solution sparingly, and remove the excess with a sponge or *cleaning cloth* as you go. If you own (or even better, if you can borrow from your neighbor) a *wet/dry vacuum cleaner*, it does a good job of picking up the dirty ammonia-and-water solution and saves a lot of time. Since this floor is in the bathroom where *bleach* may occasionally be used on mildew (see Question 26), we will remind you to be careful *not* to mix ammonia and bleach together; they produce a poisonous gas that can have deadly results.

After the grout is as clean as it will get, apply *grout sealer* to make cleaning at least somewhat easier the next time. This method also works for dirty grout on floors in other rooms in the home. **Opinionated Note:** If you have a chance to choose the grout color for a new floor in your home, *don't select white*. Grays, browns, tans, and so forth are much easier to maintain.

25.   White Film

After I clean the grouted tile in my bathroom, a white film spreads out over the cleaned area. What's going on?

Sounds as if the grout is dissolving. The grout was not properly applied, the grout is getting old, the cleaner is strong enough to dissolve it, or you should rinse more thoroughly. Applying a *grout sealer* will greatly slow down the dissolving process.

26.   Mildew in Grout

How do I get rid of the mildew that builds up in the white grout around the tile in my bathroom shower?

As in Question 23, first clean the grout as you clean the tiles to remove as much of the mildew as possible. Then squirt the mildewed areas with a *bleach solution* from a spray bottle. Leave the room and return in a few minutes to rinse off the bleach. Chlorine bleach kills mildew almost instantly.

If stains remain (and white grout often becomes permanently stained), a *grout coloring agent* can help. It covers up stains rather than bleaches them. The steps involved are: Clean the grout, seal it (see Question 25), and then recolor it. The coloring product has its own applicator. Apply it, let it dry, and then wipe off any excess. Don't use this product on floors because it won't stay white very long, or on working countertops because of the various stain-producing spills that happen there. But it works well on shower walls. It cannot fix grout that is not there. That's up to you.

27.　Mildew Prevention

How do I reduce the amount of mildew in the bathroom?

Just like the old movie monsters that scared us as kids, mildew thrives in damp, dark, misty conditions. Short of the monster's foggy swamp, your bathroom couldn't be more perfect as a home for mildew. Here are some suggestions, however, to chase away mildew demons lurking in your bathroom:

1.　Keep surfaces clean. Dirt, grease, body oils, and so forth are all like Thanksgiving dinner to mildew.
2.　Keep a *squeegee* in the shower, and use it on the shower walls, door, and floor after showering. Towel them dry after squeegeeing in extreme cases.
3.　Leave the shower door open or the shower curtains parted after you're done showering.
4.　Open a window to keep fresh air circulating.

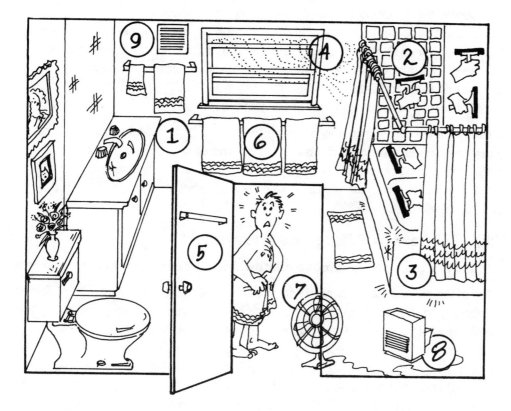

5. Leave the bathroom door ajar during showering.
6. Hang the towels so they will dry completely before the next day's use.
7. Put a portable fan in the bathroom, and turn it on after showering to help exchange wet bathroom air for drier air from other rooms.
8. Get a dehumidifier.
9. Get really serious and install an exhaust fan.

Note: When building a home, install windows in the bathroom that are at least as big as windows in the other rooms of the house. Clear glass will make the room more appealing. If privacy is an issue, use the same window covering that you use on windows in other rooms—except for miniblinds. (See Question 87).

28. Mildew in Fiberglass Showers

What's the best way to remove mildew from a fiberglass shower?

Most mildew will be removed via weekly cleaning, using standard *Speed Cleaning* methods. In other words, apply *fiberglass cleaner*, agitate with a *white pad* and a *toothbrush*, and then rinse. This will remove *soap scum* and water spots, and it will also remove most or all of the mildew. If mildew remains, apply household liquid *bleach solution.* Use a spray bottle to do this, but adjust the nozzle so it squirts, rather than sprays, the bleach onto the mildew. This minimizes the amount of bleach in the air that you might breathe. (Also leave a window open if you can.) Leave the room immediately after applying the bleach, close the door if you don't appreciate bleach odor in the rest of the house, and return a few minutes later for a final rinse with cool or warm (not hot) water. Rinsing is not optional; chlorine bleach can eat away at chrome fixtures and other durable surfaces if left to its own devices. Grout, especially older grout, can begin to dissolve as well. **Note:** This method works for tile showers also.

29. Fiberglass Showers

I scratched a fiberglass shower in our last house. I'm a bit gun shy about cleaning the fiberglass where we now live. Please give me some guidelines (and confidence).

Try using *Red Juice* and a *cleaning cloth* only. If the fiberglass is fairly new and still nice and smooth, that may be all you need to keep it clean. If necessary, you can use Soft Scrub or Bon Ami occasionally, but not regularly, for heavy *soap scum*. If you have *hard-water spot* problems, it's okay to use *Tile Juice* or Lime-A-Way or other acidic cleaners. Rinse thoroughly.

For tough stains such as adhesive residue, tar, and paint, you can use a light *solvent* like lighter fluid or paint thinner. Don't use any more than is necessary, and don't let the solvent contact any plastics. When finished, wipe away any remaining solvent with Red Juice and a cleaning cloth.

30.   Hard-Water Spots on Glass Shower Doors

My glass shower doors are cloudy even after I've cleaned them with Tile Juice and the tile brush. I know we have very hard water, but what can I do?

It's time to up the ante. One of the *Speed Cleaning* rules says: "If what you're doing isn't working, then shift to a heavier-duty cleaner or tool." In this case, shift to a *white pad*, possibly to a razor in a razor holder, or even to #0000 steel wool. (Before using the razor or steel wool, test them in that legendary *inconspicuous spot*. Some shower doors that appear to be glass may actually be plastic, and the razor or steel wool will scratch plastic.)

Another approach is to increase the amount of time the Tile Juice works on the *hard-water spots* before you go to work with these tools. Apply the Tile Juice, and allow it to soften the hard-water deposits by chemical action for five or ten minutes. Rewet the area with Tile Juice a couple of times, if necessary. Use a *scraper* to remove mineral deposits where the tub and the shower door-frame meet. If a metal scraper leaves black marks, remove them with cleanser or use a plastic scraper instead. Once you do get it clean, I suggest that whoever takes the last shower of the morning and evening *squeegee* the shower doors and walls dry. (See Question 31.)

31.   Clear Shower Door

After I've worked so hard to get it clean, my clear shower door gets dirty the instant I use the shower again. What's going on?

Hard-water spots are a lot easier to prevent than to remove. Do this by squeegeeing away water that would otherwise dry and leave deposits. Hang a *squeegee* in each shower and make a new house rule: The last person to take a shower *must* use the squeegee to dry the shower walls and door. It takes just a few moments, but it will make a big difference. The shower walls, and especially a clear shower door, will stay clean longer and will be a lot easier to clean next time. If you have particularly hard water, take one more step, and wipe with a towel to remove any residual water after squeegeeing. If you take this short additional step, you won't have to clean the shower at all for weeks or months at a time!

32.   Clogged Shower Head

My shower head is clogged with hard-water deposits. I got the bright idea of using toothpicks to jab into the openings, but they just broke off, and now I'm having a hard time getting the toothpick remains out. How can I clear the nozzle openings?

To remove the hard-water accumulation, soak the shower head overnight in a solution of one part white *vinegar* and two parts water. Dislodge the loosened deposits with a *toothbrush*. Repeat if necessary. If you have a detachable shower head on a hose, you don't even have to remove the shower head. Just set a bowl of vinegar and water solution below the shower head, and soak it in the bowl. Otherwise, it requires a wrench to remove the shower head. Avoid scratching the chrome by putting a *cleaning cloth* or tape between the shower head and the wrench.

Remove the broken and stuck toothpicks with tweezers or needle-nose pliers.

33. Preventing Hard-Water Spots

It seems I spend half my life fighting hard-water spots. Is there a permanent solution that's legal?

Yes. Install a water softener. Besides the visible *hard-water spots* on showers and elsewhere, hard water promotes soap deposits, scaly deposits in plumbing and appliances, and impaired cleaning action of soaps and detergents. Hard water's one good characteristic? It usually tastes better than soft water.

34.   Soap Scum

What do I use to clean heavy soap scum from bathroom tile?

A heavy-duty liquid cleaner such as *Red Juice* should get it off. Manufacturers are fond of intimating that it takes a special cleaner to combat *soap scum*. It doesn't. Let the cleaner soak in for a longer period, and use a *tile brush* or a *white pad* with extra vigor. Resort to a razor blade in a holder if necessary, but the soap scum will come off without too much of a struggle.

Hard-water spots are much more tenacious. If your efforts weren't successful, it could be that you're confusing soap scum with hard-water deposits. The way to tell the difference is to scratch the afflicted area with your fingernail. Soap scum will collect under your fingernail and feel waxy. Hard-water deposits will stay put. (If the culprit is the latter, use *Tile Juice* instead of Red Juice, and see Question 30.)

35.   Brass Fixtures

Is there a strong cleaner that I can use on a shower door if there is brass instead of chrome around the door?

You can't safely use a strong cleaner on brass that has a coating of clear lacquer on its surface. (See Questions 54 and 55.) Most brass bathroom fixtures have such a coating. Abrasive cleaners will scratch, damage, or remove sections of the lacquer. Those areas will then promptly tarnish. *Gently* clean with *Red Juice* or *Blue Juice* and a *cleaning cloth.*

Use brass polish *only* if the brass isn't protected with a lacquer coating. (Apply the brass polish after routine cleaning.) Even if it's uncoated brass, powdered cleansers will scratch the brass and make it difficult to achieve a good shine. As you can tell, brass is tricky in bathrooms! So is gold, for that matter, but if you own gold bathroom fixtures, you probably aren't the one who cleans them.

36. Nonslip Strips

It's time to replace the grungy, worn-out, half-missing nonslip strips in my tub, but when I tried to pull the old ones off, I couldn't do it. Should I add new ones on top of the old ones?

No. If you double them up, the new ones won't adhere properly. The outside layer of those strips is impervious to almost all cleaning agents, so try to remove the top layer or two of the strip mechanically. Start by prying up one corner with a plastic spatula or fingernail. Try another corner if your first choice is holding tight. Or warm up the sticker with a hair dryer to soften the adhesive. **Note:** A gentle heating softens the adhesive on many products, including tape, labels, and price tags.

Once you're down to the sticky residue (what's left after you get rid of the strip itself) use a *solvent* like *De-Zov-All* or lighter fluid. Allow the product to sit for as long as needed to soften the adhesive. But don't wait too long or the solvent will evaporate and the adhesive will re-harden. Then rub with a *cleaning cloth,* or roll the sticker into a ball with your fingers to remove it. Clean away traces of solvent with *Red Juice* and a cleaning cloth.

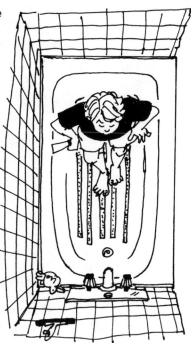

If you can't pull off the top of the strip to expose the adhesive, use the spatula to lift the edges at least a bit. Now apply the solvent and let stand for an hour or more. It may take a while, and you may have to remove the sticker in stages, but it will give up eventually. When using a solvent, use only as much as is needed, and make sure the room is well ventilated. **Note:** Before you apply new nonslip strips, prepare the surface by cleaning well with powdered cleanser. Rinse well and allow to air-dry before proceeding.

37. Acrylic Tubs/Spas

What is the best cleaner for an acrylic tub?

Acrylic tubs scratch relatively easily, but often the biggest problem is their size. Some of them are as big as a hot tub, which makes it nearly im-possible to clean them without climbing in. For cleaning, most nonabrasive cleaners are fine: e.g., *Red Juice,* Formula 409, Lime-A-Way. Rinse them away thoroughly. Avoid scouring powders like Comet or even Soft Scrub. Nor should you use a *white pad,* a green pad, steel wool, or a metal *scraper.* A *soft-bristled brush* on a swivel handle can allow you to do the cleaning without the risk of climbing into the slippery tub itself. **Note 1:** Since acrylic tubs, hot tubs, and spas are so easy to scratch, the secret is never to let them get very dirty. Regular maintenance isn't an option if you want to keep the surface looking good. If you fall behind, it's nearly impossible to clean as aggressively as needed without damaging the acrylic surface. **Note 2:** Acrylic surfaces respond well to protective wax products and specialized sealants such as *Bathroom Barrier.* Applying the protectant means an extra step, but dirt, *soap scum,* and *hard-water spots* can't cling to it as tightly as they can to the acrylic itself, making them all easier to remove. (See Question 5.)

38. Shower Curtains

Any good suggestions for speed-cleaning shower curtains?

We have two good ones. (1) Put the shower curtain in the washing machine. Throw in a couple of towels, and use warm water. Remove it before the spin cycle. (It won't be hurt if it goes through the spin cycle; it will just be very wrinkled.) Warm the curtain only slightly in the dryer (don't run the full cycle), and it will emerge close to wrinkle free. If you don't put it in the dryer, wrinkles will slowly disappear after the curtain is rehung. (2) Buy a beautiful cloth shower curtain of whatever design appeals to you. Line it with the cheapest plain white shower curtain you can find (about six dollars). If you trim the liner so that its hem falls about halfway between the top and the bottom of the tub, it will stay cleaner longer. When the liner starts to look dirty (in about six months), recycle it and install a brand new, sparkling-clean liner. Twelve dollars a year seems a small price to pay to us, but if it doesn't seem that way to you, just wash them as above. **Note:** Use only a white shower liner (or shower curtain if you have no liner) because that is the color of most *hard-water spots* and *soap scum*. Clear is the most laborious choice by far.

39. Resurfaced Tubs

We just moved into a house that has two resurfaced tubs. We learned this from the real estate agent, but he couldn't furnish us with cleaning instructions. I have heard these tubs require special care. What do you guys recommend?

Here's the scoop. Naturally, the new surface won't be as durable as the original porcelain, so such relatively strong cleansers as Ajax and Comet shouldn't be used. *Pro-Scrub*, Bon Ami, and Soft Scrub are fine. Also avoid harsh chemicals that can react with the new surface, such as Tilex and

X-14. Use *Red Juice* instead. Don't leave a rubber bath mat in the tub all the time. Take it out between uses, or it may bond with the new surface. And be aware that if you install nonslip strips, they can *never* be removed without damaging the new surface.

## 40.	Bath Mat Stain

My bath mat left a colored stain on my linoleum floor that I can't get up. Any ideas?

Yes, but we must be gentle in the telling of them. Some stains are permanent, and a stain that involves a transfer of dye from the mat or from the backing of the mat to a linoleum floor falls squarely in the permanent category. Linoleum is an almost extinct floor material that is more porous than tile or vinyl. We're not being cruel, merely truthful, when we say replace the floor, or cover the stain with a new mat.

## 41.	Cultured Marble

Since they cost about as much as I paid for my first car, I'm keenly motivated to know how to clean our new Corian countertops.

They are beautiful, but they are dear. They are also a bit sensitive, so don't use anything abrasive. They can react to acids, so don't use an acidic cleaner like *Tile Juice*. Instead apply *fiberglass cleaner*, *Red Juice*, or *marble polish* with a *toothbrush*, *cleaning cloth*, or a *polishing cloth*. Spray the surface liberally if you are using fiberglass cleaner or Red Juice, and get into the corners to loosen difficult dirt with the toothbrush (gently). Otherwise, wipe them clean and dry with a cleaning cloth. If you are using marble polish, apply it with a polishing cloth. Move items on the counter from left to right to clean an area, then replace the items before starting the next part of the counter. Help protect the surface by applying a coat of *Bathroom Barrier*.

42. Streaky Mirrors

Is there a surefire way to keep mirrors from streaking when I clean them?

The secret to streak-free mirrors is to wipe them with a very dry *cleaning cloth* until they are completely dry. This usually means a few swipes beyond the point when you think you are done. You're probably wiping them with a cloth that is slightly damp and leaves just a bit of moisture on the surface. As that dries, it leaves traces of the cleaning solution as a streak.

If you still have streaks after drying the surface completely, dilute the glass cleaner with water. If the glass cleaner is more dilute, it's easier to wipe away without leaving a streak. Also, as when washing windows, never clean a mirror in the sun.

43. Hair Spray

Depending on whether I'm applying hair spray to the front or back of my hair, I get the spray on the mirror or a framed, glass-covered picture. Red Juice has finally met its match. How do I get the hair spray off?

Hair spray is lacquer. That's why it's difficult to remove. But rubbing alcohol, something you probably have right there in the bathroom, will remove it. Pour rubbing alcohol on a *cleaning cloth* or paper towel and wipe until the hair spray dissolves and is removed. Wipe with a dry cleaning cloth or spray with *Blue Juice,* and wipe dry to finish the job. It's safest not to spray Blue Juice directly on the front of the picture. It could damage the print and cause a stain if liquid is wicked up between the glass and the painting. **Note:** Stand elsewhere when spritzing your hair. You know where your hair is, so standing in front of the mirror isn't absolutely essential. Once you have your hair properly coiffed, take a step or two back or to the side before spritzing.

44. Toilet Rings

Toilet-bowl rings are driving me crazy!

I'm going to assume that that is a question. I also assume you've tried all manner of standard cleaning methods, including liquid bleaches, pow-

dered cleanser, and *Tile Juice.* The solution may seem drastic, but it's safe and effective: a *pumice stick.* Pumice is a mild abrasive that's softer than porcelain (so it doesn't scratch it) but harder than the toilet ring (so it can rub it off). Make sure both the porcelain and the pumice stick are wet before starting, and then gently rub off the ring with the stick. You'll be amazed. If this is a persistent problem, think about installing a water softener. **Note:** Toilet rings, which are caused by water evaporating and leaving behind tenacious mineral deposits, can cause permanent damage if ignored for long periods of time. If the stains aren't removed by pumice and the porcelain surface is uneven in that area, you may have to replace the toilet itself to solve the problem!

45.   Rusty Toilet Bowls

I'm embarrassed to let company use the bathroom because of rust stains in the toilet bowls. I'm running out of excuses! What should I do?

How nice of you to give your company such a lively topic of conversation for the trip home! As you might expect, rust stains are usually due to iron in the water. Iron can also stain the laundry and add an unpleasant taste to the water. The most commonly used chemical to remove rust is oxalic acid. Examples of products with oxalic acid are *Rust Remover*, Bar Keepers Friend, and Zud. Oxalic acid is toxic, so follow the manufacturer's directions respectfully and completely. Don't use chlorine *bleach* on rust because it sets the stain and makes your problem worse. Another solution is to install an iron filter in the water line. Lastly, it's possible that your porcelain toilet has worn so thin over the years that the underlying metal is now exposed to water and is rusting. In this case it's definitely time for a replacement.

Blue, green, or other unusual stains may be the result of corrosion or long-term cleaning with abrasive cleaners. They may be permanent. Chlorine bleach, peroxide, and oxalic acid products can lighten these stains, but you're probably better off replacing the fixture.

46. Oak Toilet Seat

How should I clean my oak toilet seat?

Just remind yourself that you're not cleaning the oak itself; you're cleaning the plastic finish. Therefore, go right ahead and use *Red Juice* or whatever liquid cleaner you use on the other surfaces in your bathroom. Don't forget a *toothbrush* in and around all those annoying hinges and rubber bumpers.

47. Missed Targets

How do you get human urine out of the tile grout in the bathroom floors?

Rewet the area with *Red Juice*. Use *cleaning cloths* or paper towels to soak up as much as you can. Now spray with an *enzyme cleaner* like Stain Gobbler. Enzymes are proteins that will break down the organic remains of the urine. This process also removes the source of any lingering odors. (See Question 23.)

48.   Disinfecting Toilet Bowls

What do you recommend for disinfecting toilet bowls?

Cleaning a toilet bowl by scrubbing with a *toilet brush* and a cleanser removes or kills nearly all bacteria. For a more complete disinfection, (1) use a powdered cleanser that contains bleach; (2) pour household chlorine *bleach* directly into the toilet bowl (a half cup is plenty), swish it around the bowl, let it stand for five to ten minutes, then flush; or (3) purchase a specialized disinfectant. (For more about disinfection in the home, see Questions 146 and 148.)

49.   Teenagers

How do you get teenagers to help clean the bathroom? I'm trying to teach mine that it doesn't take two hours, but it does take more than two minutes.

We salute your determination and wish you great success. Learning how to clean is an essential part of the skills required to get along in life. After all, cleaning skills can ease your toil, save time, and result in a more enjoyable living space for the rest of a lifetime. Also, even though your children may not realize it right now (or admit it if they do!), most people find a task more enjoyable once they know how to do it properly and are skillful at it—no matter what the skill is.

In order for teenagers to warm to the prospect of doing their share of cleaning, you might have a fighting chance if they realize they're getting it over with in absolutely the least time possible (this also shows you're respecting their time and interests). As you are no doubt keenly aware, teenagers are in a developmental stage when absolute rules become less and less effective. Adults relate to one another far more often with contracts (agreements) than with rules. So if you can approach your teenagers on more of a contractual basis, you might get a better response—something in the order of "We have a contract: I'll give you an allowance in exchange for meeting certain conditions." You're looking for what's called a meeting of the minds. Our *Speed Cleaning* techniques, in book or video form, teach someone how to clean any room in a fast, step-by-step, easy-to-learn manner. They cover how to divide up the work (in a team effort, if possible), where to start each job, and what tools to use—from Step 1 to Step 2 to completion. I don't want to get your hopes too high, but they have worked for thousands of other families. Oh, you will undoubtedly also need a reward. **Note:** Similar tactics also work for adults. For example, if someone just plain doesn't like cleaning and is avoiding it, learning how to do it really helps! A big

reason people dislike a task is because they're not exactly sure how to go about it. Learn Speed Cleaning, be done with the cleaning and the guilt, and move on.

50.   Cleaning Alone

I need an ally. I work all the time. It doesn't much matter whether I'm at home or the office, there's always more to do than I can seemingly ever get done. Not only housecleaning, but cooking, shopping, transporting kids, helping with homework, patting the dog and my husband on the head, and on and on and on. Is this fair?

No, and it's dangerous too. In her book *The Second Shift: Working Parents and the Revolution at Home*, Arlie Hochschild, sociologist and author, calls a woman like you who tries to do everything the superwoman. It's not possible to do it all. There's just not enough time. There are other prices to pay. Divorce is one of them.

My opinion is that if both spouses are working, a division of labor at home, not biased by gender-specific job definitions, is imperative. It may be that one spouse does all the housework but the other spouse does the shopping and transporting of the kids, for example. Talk to your husband, and negotiate a fairer division of labor at home. If your kids are old enough, or as they get older, recruit them to help also. After all, they contribute most to getting the house dirty. They should help clean it. See Question 49 for ideas on how to teach cleaning skills to the uninitiated majority in your family. **Note:** It's only because the questioner is a woman that the answer is restricted to problems faced by her sex. In fact men are faced with changing and seemingly impossible time demands day in and day out as well. The solution, putting aside historic gender-specific traditions about who should do what, is to develop in each household as fair a division of labor as you can sort out together.

Chapter 4

OTHER ROOMS

51. White Rings

I don't seem to be able to remove a white ring on my antique coffee table. It appeared after someone left a hot coffee cup on it. Help!

If you think coffee rings are bad, try to imagine what a table looks like after three hot pizzas have been left on it. Pizza rings! (The fact that this happened at *The Clean Team* headquarters was all the more distressing.) Then there was the time my grandmother decided to cool a batch of cookies on the dining-room table. Thirty-six utterly charming and sentimental cookie rings were left behind as an heirloom for her grandchildren.

What most furniture rings have in common is that moisture has become trapped in the finish. It's a sort of permanent fog. If you can coax the moisture out with an appropriate restorative (e.g., *Furniture Feeder*, Howard Restor-A-Finish), the ring will vanish before your eyes. Shake the product well, and then pour a small amount on the spot or the *polishing cloth* according to product directions. Rub a small area of the ring gently but firmly with the polishing cloth. It's safest to rub back and forth with the grain of the wood, but try any combination, including against the grain, to remove the ring. After some moments—from a few to quite a few—that segment of the ring should start to fade and then disappear. If such is the case, continue as directed until the entire ring vanishes. If not, try the same procedure, only with paste wax this time.

If these preliminary skirmishes didn't work, hold your breath and apply the restorative with #0000 steel wool instead of the polishing cloth. A word of caution: Intensive rubbing with either the polishing cloth or the steel wool can start to destroy the finish on many antiques, depending on the type of finish, its age, and its overall condition. Be sure to test that legendary *inconspicuous spot* first. Yes, I know that spot doesn't have a ring on it, but just test to be sure that you aren't damaging the finish with the cloth and *solvent,* and test it again if you up the ante to steel wool. **Note:** I know it isn't easy, but don't be shy about offering coasters to your guests. It will save you from repeating this chore.

52. Artificial Plants

My mother-in-law has given me several silk plants over the years. I must confess that I've neglected them. What's the best way to dust them?

The fastest way is to use the brush attachment of a vacuum. If the vacuum isn't effective alone, use it along with a handheld *dusting brush*. If the dirt on the silk plant is sticky and can't be removed by these methods, add a small amount of dishwashing soap to a sinkful of warm water, and *gently* swish the plant in the solution. Rinse *gently* with clean warm water and allow to air-dry. (Of course, first test for colorfastness on a potential candidate for martyrdom.) **Note:** Some things are nonmaintainable. If your artificial plant is dirty, can't be satisfactorily dusted, or fails the *inconspicuous spot* test, it's time to toss it unless it's politically incorrect if your mother-in-law notices its disappearance.

53. Dried Plants

I have a beautiful dried plant and flower arrangement. At least it used to be beautiful. Now it's covered with dust and cobwebs, not to mention broken flower petals, leaves, stems, et cetera.

When you first install a dried flower arrangement or wreath in your home, start dusting it carefully and attentively with a feather duster as you clean your way around the room. This will remove cobwebs and some of the dust.

But dried flower arrangements by their nature are too delicate to withstand rigorous cleaning methods. And accidents will inevitably befall them: flowers will fall off, twigs will snap, and so on. Accordingly, dried flower arrangements have fairly short life spans. It may be too late for this particular arrangement, but if you have one that is cherished, consider having a clear plastic dustcover made for it at a plastics shop. They're not very expensive, they're considerably easier to dust, and you can still enjoy the appearance of the plants. Otherwise, no matter how beautiful they once were and no matter how expensive they were when purchased, dried plants should not be considered heirlooms to be passed from generation to generation.

54. Brass Discoloration

How do you get discoloration out of brass?

Boy, do we get a lot of questions on brass. Let's get them all cleared up once and for all. There are two possible situations: **The brass is coated with clear lacquer**. Lacquer keeps the brass from being exposed to the air and tarnishing as a result. So long as the lacquer coating remains intact, the brass will look newly polished. Clean it by dusting or wiping it with a damp cloth. Unfortunately the lacquer can eventually (perhaps inevitably) peel or wear off. Just like paint, it gets nicked here and there, or the coating gets wiped or rubbed or scratched off during cleaning. Once the lacquer coating is compromised, the area of brass exposed to the air starts to tarnish while the rest of the brass stays shiny. That's when we get questions about discoloration. There's no satisfactory solution to this condition other than: (a) Remove the rest of the lacquer with a paint stripper safe for use on metals. (Examples are 3M's Safest Stripper and Jasco's Speedomatic.) Then clean and polish the brass, and apply new coats of lacquer. Specialized (i.e., very expensive) clear lacquer in spray cans is available in many upscale hardware or paint stores. Be warned, however, that relacquering is a *very* tricky thing to do properly at home: Dust gets trapped in the lacquer, the lacquer runs, et cetera. (b) Remove the rest of the lacquer, polish the brass, and forget about relacquering. You will have to repolish it every so often for the rest of your life, until you sell it at a garage sale or until you decide that a little tarnish adds to its charm. (c) Pay a metal refinisher to strip and relacquer it for you. (Look in the yellow pages under "Plating" or "Metal Refinishing.") **Note:** The secret of owning good-looking lacquered brass is to handle and clean it as gently as you would an egg. Take extreme precautions to ensure that nothing happens to nick, to scratch, or otherwise to remove even the tiniest bit of lacquer, because that's when the "discoloration" will start again.

The brass has no protective coating. In this case the brass tarnishes uniformly. It will take on a darker and darker shade as the tarnish gets more and more established. Fingerprints show up startlingly well as the tarnish develops. The solution is to polish it with a brass polish as often as you must to keep it satisfactorily shiny. You always have the option of coating it with lacquer, but then you will have Problem 1 above. Oh, well.

55. Brass Sconces

I'm quite proud of my matching brass sconces. What can I use to clean them?

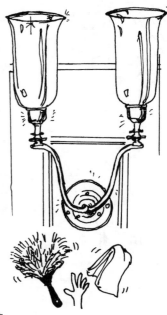

Most sconces are protected against tarnishing by a lacquer coating, as are most brass knickknacks. (See Question 54.) So, most of the time clean them with only a feather duster. When the duster isn't effective, wipe them gently with a *cleaning cloth* dampened with *Blue Juice* or water. Then go back to feather dusting for as long as you can before the brass needs to be hand-wiped again.

56. Brass Film

My new brass fixtures have a film over them. How can I/should I take it off?

Leave it alone. It's the lacquer coating referred to in the previous two questions. It's conceivable that your fixtures were covered with a thick plastic film to protect them during shipping, but that should be easy to peel off.

57. Lampshades

Over time my lampshades have slowly gotten darker and darker. I must admit that I don't clean them. Should I? With what?

Yes, you should, because lampshades with their rough and complex surfaces are particularly good dust catchers. Get rid of the current serious accumulation with a *dusting brush*. Then routinely use a feather duster or the brush attachment of a vacuum during during regular cleaning sessions.

58. Water-Stained Vase

My favorite glass vase is terribly stained. I know the stains come from water evaporating when there are flowers in the vase. What I don't know is how to get rid of them. Help. I love my vase, but I hate the stains.

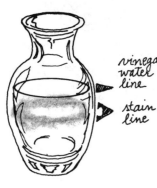

vinegar water line

stain line

This is one case when the put-it-in-the-dishwasher rule doesn't work. The dishwasher does a fine job of cleaning the outside of a vase but of course completely misses the inside. Instead pour enough white *vinegar* and water (1:1 ratio) into the vase to cover the stain line. Allow it to stand for several hours or overnight. Before emptying, insert a bottle brush and scrub. Then empty and rinse. You can speed up the process considerably if you substitute *Tile Juice* for vinegar. Tile Juice is more difficult to rinse, however.

If the opening or the design of the vase won't allow a brush, pour out almost all the solution, and add a teaspoon or more (depending on the size of the vase) of uncooked rice or beans. Cover the top with your hand, and swirl and shake the vase to allow the rice or beans to rub off the loosened stain. Repeat if necessary.

59. Cleaning Ceramic Pieces

I have a ceramic frog in a suggestive pose (dressed in a painted-on bikini). Yes, it's ugly, but I love it and want to know how to clean it. It's almost impossible to clean—nothing will fit into the hard-to-reach areas.

Put your ugly-duckling-but-beloved frog into the dishwasher. If it has a hole in the bottom of it, put it in bottom side down so it won't fill up with water. If it has felt or other protectors on the bottom, you have a decision to make. You can: (1) Wash it anyway. If the protectors disappear, replace them. There are packages of protectors of all shapes and styles available at hardware stores. (2) Clean it by hand. Use Q-Tips or a soft brush along with a cleaner such as *Red Juice* to reach into all those places you can't otherwise get to.

60. Paintings

How do you clean an original oil painting that has no glass protecting it?

Much depends on the value of the painting. If it's an original Caravaggio, run to the phone and call a professional conservator or restorer. But if it's an original by dear Aunt Bessie, occasioned by her first art class, that's a different story.

This is tricky business, however, and something we have little experience with, so we turned to a professional conservator of paintings—Carolyn Tallent, from Santa Monica, California—for her wise counsel. She advises: (1) Inspect every square inch of the surface—in search of loose or flaking paint, hairline cracks, or other damage. If any are present, take the painting to a pro. (2) Remove the painting to a flat surface or lean it against a wall where you can work on it without fear of its falling. (3) Dust the surface. As Carolyn observes, you can imagine what a hallway mirror would look like if you hadn't dusted it for several years. That's the sort of schmutz your painting is covered with. So—how to dust? The trick is to use a soft brush. Some paintbrushes are too stiff; choose a natural-bristle brush with feathered tips or, even better, a soft camel-hair brush available at art supply stores. She suggests dedicating this brush for dusting your paintings only. (4) If the dust deposits are heavy, hold the long-nosed nozzle attachment of the vacuum cleaner a couple of inches from the surface as you work so the dust doesn't resettle. (5) Stop after a thorough dusting because further cleaning with water is fraught with disastrous possibilities. However, if the painting has no great value, if you feel like living dangerously, and if the painting needs further cleaning, roll (not rub) cotton swabs lightly dampened with plain water over the surface. Don't use *any* type of soap or household cleaner. If the painting has sentimental value, or if the monetary value of the painting is unknown, don't go beyond dusting.

61. Furniture Wax Buildup

What is the best way to remove wax buildup from wood furniture?

Certain restorative *solvents*, such as *Furniture Feeder*, dissolve wax buildup. Apply the solvent to a disposable *polishing cloth* or directly to the furniture (pretest). Loosen and remove the old wax with the polishing cloth, assisted by a *toothbrush* in nooks and crannies (check first to be sure that the toothbrush doesn't scratch the finish). During the removal phase you can position the toothbrush over the cloth so the bristles poke the cloth into these same nooks and crannies. **Note:** In the future don't use wax on the intricate parts of wood furniture for more than one coat. Rewax only the flat tops and occasionally the flat sides.

62.   Marble Bar

We just moved into a new house with a beautiful marble bar-top. There are stains on it that look like glass rings. I've tried everything to get them out, but I'm afraid of using something too harsh. Do you have any suggestions?

First try a combination *marble polish* and cleaner—or good old *Red Juice*. Apply either, and wipe well. I assume you've tried this, so let's move on. You might also try leaving the polish and cleaner on the ring for several hours before wiping.

I've had great luck removing hard-to-remove things from marble with a razor blade. First wet the surface with Red Juice, and gently scrape with the blade at a low angle. Use a fresh single-edge razor in a holder. Stone International (Florence, Italy) says light rings or stains can be removed by applying a small amount of hydrogen peroxide or clear *ammonia*. Use #0000 steel wool, if necessary, "with a very light hand." (We suggest consulting a professional *before* having at it with steel wool.) At the very least, pretest. Afterward wipe clean, let dry, and, Stone International suggests, apply a wax such as Johnson's paste wax.

Discouraging Note: Marble can last for centuries (just ask the Romans), but it is porous enough to stain and is remarkably vulnerable to acids. Unfortunately a great number of drinks are acidic (e.g., wine, citrus juices, colas, cranberry juice, and tomato juice). The same is true of fruits often found near a bar (e.g., lemons, limes, and oranges). So it's likely that something acidic has etched its way into the surface as a permanent feature. If so, it's not dirt at all, and no manner of cleaning will prevail against it. It's time to consult a professional who will work over the area with a buffer and a pumice or rottenstone abrasive. In the meantime immediately wipe off *anything* spilled (rinse if the spill is acidic), and don't allow beverage glasses to be set directly on the marble.

63. Candle Wax

I love candles on the table at dinnertime, but I hate trying to remove the wax from the table afterward. At the moment I hate the cleanup more than I love the candlelight. How do you remove the candle wax without destroying the candlelight experience?

Here's how to restore that candlelight ambience to your life. To remove candle wax from the table itself, first scrape 95 percent of it off with a plastic *scraper*. The wax will come off in chunks if it's cool, and it will peel off if it's warm. To collect the loosened wax, use either a whisk broom and dustpan,

or a vacuum cleaner with the plastic nozzle attachment. You will get good at this and learn how to remove practically all the wax in just a few minutes. The second step is to spray the remaining bit of wax with furniture polish and wipe it off with a *polishing cloth* as you're polishing the entire tabletop. If and when furniture polish builds up, treat the table top with *Furniture Feeder.* (See Question 1.)

You didn't mention them, but the candlesticks can be cleaned approximately the same way. While holding a candlestick over a trash can or newspapers, use the same plastic scraper to remove most of the wax. Warm, soapy water and a sponge will remove the rest. **Note 1:** Remove candle wax from a tablecloth using the same warm-iron-and-paper-towel method described in Question 66, except now you can put paper towels on both sides. Pour a little liquid soap on the spot and launder as usual. **Note 2:** A glass ring called a bobeche (bo-BESH) slips over the candle, sits at its base, and catches most of the wax before it drips onto the table. It's found at good hardware stores and is downright cheap.

64. Crayon Art

How do you remove crayon marks from painted walls and wallpapered walls? Sigh.

Use lighter fluid, *De-Zov-All*, WD-40, or another mild *solvent* and a *toothbrush* to remove most of the crayon from the wall. Spray or wipe with the solvent and then, ever so gently, brush with the toothbrush. Use a *cleaning cloth* to blot away residue. Finally, spray and wipe the area with *Red Juice* to remove the last traces of crayon and solvent. Follow the same procedure on wallpaper after first testing for colorfastness and the effects of the solvent and Red Juice in that legendary *inconspicuous place*. Naturally, you should avoid saturating the wallpaper as well as scrubbing too hard with the toothbrush or cloths. **Next best bet:** If the solvent fails the inconspicuous-spot test or isn't effective, try paper towels and a warm iron. (See Question 66.)

65. Cleaning Wallpaper

What do you use for general cleaning of wallpaper?

Occasional removal of dust with a cloth or by vacuuming is all the general cleaning that's called for. Smudges and other small marks can be removed with a gum *eraser*. See other questions for specifics such as the removal of crayon marks, grease, et cetera.

66. Grease and Wallpaper

Grease stains have mysteriously appeared on my wallpaper, and no one is fessing up. I'll solve the mystery eventually and get my revenge, but in the meantime how do you remove grease from wallpaper?

Most greasy fingerprints can be removed with *Red Juice*, a *cleaning cloth*, and gentle encouragement with a *toothbrush* (pretest). For larger grease spots, place a few white paper towels folded to cover the grease stain. Press the paper towels with a warm iron until the grease is absorbed into the paper towels. Keep turning the towels to a fresh area, or replacing them.

67. Poster Stuck on Wall

How do I get a poster off the wall, that got wet and stuck to the paint after a water-balloon fight?

Am I talking to a penitent participant (I hope) or to the parent cleaning up after the war? (I'm so sorry.) In either case the solution is relatively easy. The secret to getting the poster off is to rehydrate it—that is, to get it wet again. Spray it several times with plain water, until it is soaked, and wait a few moments. You should then be able to pull it off the wall. Encouragement with a plastic *scraper* or spatula may be needed. It may leave some stains or other residue that should come off with *Red Juice* and a *cleaning cloth*. If ink transferred to the wall, you may have to dab on a *bleach solution* (chlorine or peroxide) and rinse, provided the wall surface will tolerate it. A water balloon fight, huh?

68. Nicotine on Walls

How do I get nicotine off painted surfaces?

Nicotine comes off most surfaces nicely with a dilute clear *ammonia* solution or *Red Juice.* If the painted surfaces are cabinets, baseboards, window frames, and so forth, just spray with Red Juice and wipe with a *cleaning cloth.* Use a *toothbrush* to reach into corners.

If the painted surfaces are walls and ceilings, mix clear ammonia in a bucket (start with about one part ammonia to ten parts water and make it stronger only if needed). Apply with a *flat mop* or a large sponge. Wipe first with either one, and then dry with a cleaning cloth or dry *flat mop* cover. **Discouraging Note:** If the surfaces are covered with flat paint and the paint and the nicotine stains are old, you may have to repaint. But wash them anyway to get rid of at least some of the odor. And ask your paint supplier how best to seal or prime the surface before repainting to avoid possible bleed-through of those lovely nicotine stains.

69. Soot on Walls

The wall above my fireplace has noticeable amounts of black soot. What should I do?

If you're lucky, you'll get some of it off just by vacuuming with the brush attachment. For the hard-core soot that's remaining, there are specialized soot cleaners (e.g., Red Devil and one a chimney sweep I know swears by, Speedy White) available in most hardware stores, but I would just as soon use clear dilute *ammonia solution*. It's safe, effective, and substantially less expensive. Use a *flat mop* or large sponge and *cleaning cloths* to wash the wall itself. Dip a mop cover or sponge into the cleaning solution, wring it out almost dripping wet, and clean an area of the wall. Use a second, dry mop cover or cleaning cloth to dry each clean area before you move on. **Note:** Soot on small, smooth areas can often be removed with a large *eraser.*

Brick walls covered with soot respond well to cleaning with trisodium phosphate (up to one-half cup in a gallon of hot water) or Speedy White and a handheld brush. Dry with cleaning cloths. It would be wise to seal brick or stone walls near fireplaces to resist future absorption of grease and soot. **One other thing:** This wall will not come perfectly clean very many times, so fix the fireplace; the draft is too slow, the chimney needs cleaning, or something else is askew.

70. Fireplace Bricks

How do you clean the bricks *in* a fireplace?

If you're talking about the bricks that form the sides and floor of the fireplace, the answer is, you don't; you just ignore them. If you're talking about the bricks that form the interior of the chimney, they are cleaned with specialized tools inserted through the top of the chimney. You must first seal the fireplace 100 percent to prevent soot from pouring out the fireplace. Try to visualize a layer of soot everywhere. Then call a chimney sweep.

71. Fingerprints

How do I clean the hundreds of fingerprints that appear on the walls of my house?

If the fingerprints are on glossy paint, they're easy to remove. So we're going to assume that the fingerprints are on flat paint. Flat paint (more so than gloss or semigloss paint) can hold on to or even absorb stains with tenacity, making the job difficult for any cleaning agent. First try to wipe the fingerprints off with *Red Juice* and a *cleaning cloth*. If the wall is particularly dirty, you may need a *white pad* or a *toothbrush*. But be careful! Even the cleaning cloth can wear away the paint beneath the fingerprints, especially if: (1) the paint is old, (2) the paint is cheap, (3) only one coat of paint had been applied, or (4) there's been a long history of scrubbing at this site.

If Red Juice doesn't work, or if the paint has been scrubbed away, the solution is to repaint. But be wily about this and repaint just what's necessary. If only the area around a switchplate is defiled, repaint only that area. Paint—especially if you have some from the same can—matches quite well for several years. If the new paint looks too different, paint up to a corner.

72. Steam Radiator

I need a nifty device or an even niftier suggestion for cleaning dust and grime out from between the tubes (or whatever they are called) of an old-fashioned steam radiator. The dustcloth-and-yardstick method is getting old, and it doesn't work anyway!

We do have something nifty for you: a *rabbit ear duster.* The "ears" of the duster can be bent into whatever shape you want, and they will stay put. Bend them to fit the part of the radiator you want to clean. Use them dry to dust, or spray them with *Red Juice* if the grunge is more serious.

73. Baby's Crib

How do you get dried baby formula off a crib's rungs? When it's caked on, it's almost like trying to remove nail polish. I haven't been able to find any way to take it off other than by scraping it off, and that's very hard to do on those round spindles. Ideas, please.

If the crib could fit in the dishwasher or if you could soak it in the bathtub for a while, the answer would be at hand. Since you can't do either of these fun things, the next best choice is to spray the encrusted areas with *Red Juice* several times over a ten- to fifteen-minute period. The idea is to rewet the baby formula to restore it almost to its original texture. Use *cleaning cloths* to catch any goop that dribbles to the bottom of the crib. When the formula is soft enough, you can wipe it off with just a cleaning cloth. If necessary, wrap a *white pad* around each rung, and *gently* scrub the formula. Try to use a cleaning cloth to catch the formula while it's still fresh. Stash a cleaning cloth near the crib for this very purpose.

74. Louvered Doors

How do I clean louvered accordion doors?

Actually no differently from other doors, only it seems more daunting and it takes longer because of all the louvers and hinges. In most cases you aren't cleaning the entire door. Spray just the fingerprints and other smudges with *Red Juice*, and wipe them with a *cleaning cloth*. Use the vacuum brush attachment to remove dust from the louvers each week or at least occasionally.

When it's time to clean the whole door, spray it with Red Juice or use a bucket with a dilute to moderate clear *ammonia solution*, and wipe it from top to bottom. Use a *toothbrush* liberally around hinges and other hard-to-reach areas, such as molding, corners, and handles, and on marks that don't come off with a cleaning cloth alone. Clean the frame around the door at the same time.

75.　Elderly Mildew

Would an enzyme product work on the elderly mildew I have on a stroller's vinyl or plastic seat cover—or not, since the stains have probably been there for four years?

(Hmm. "Elderly mildew." That's an interesting concept. How old does mildew get? We thought it lived forever, actually.) It's doubtful that the stains can be completely removed, but the mildew probably can. First wash the seat covers well. Use *Red Juice* and a *toothbrush* and really scrub: These are old stains and will resist your efforts. Then wipe with a *cleaning cloth*. Now spray with a *bleach solution*, allow it to remain five minutes, and then rinse with abundant water. You can apply an *enzyme cleaner* like Stain Gobbler instead of bleach if you prefer.

76.　Mildew Lurking in the Closet

My daughter lives in La Jolla, California, which is quite humid. Mold turns up in weird places in her apartment. It grows on the closet walls. It attacks shoes, clothes, et cetera. We've bought the bags of crystals to take the hu-

midity out of the air, and she's made a mixture of water, bleach, and trisodium phosphate, and she cleans regularly. Any suggestions? Any products?

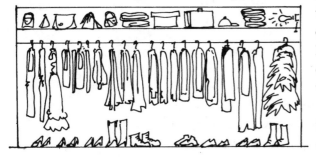

Chlorine *bleach* is the best and cheapest mildew fighter. If the walls are dirty besides being mildewy, first wash them with a dilute *ammonia solution*, and then wipe them dry with a *cleaning cloth*. Depending on the surface, the paint, and other factors, this may also remove the mildew. If not, wipe the mildew with a *bleach solution*, and wipe again with a wet cloth to remove most of the bleach. **WARNING:** Don't mix the ammonia and bleach or use bleach before the ammonia has been wiped off and the walls are dry. Bleach and ammonia together are dangerous. If you prefer not to smell ammonia in such small quarters, trisodium phosphate or *Red Juice* will also work well.

To discourage the mildew from returning, keep the closet as clean and dry as possible. Leave the door open. Mildew loves dirt, so store only clean clothes and clean shoes in the closet. Allow space between clothes and shoes. (If the closet is overflowing, see *Clutter Control* [New York: Dell] for a step-by-step plan for solving that problem.) Brush mildew off shoes regularly. Keep a light on in the closet for several hours a day or even continuously during the season when mildew growth is greatest. If it lacks both a light and an outlet, buy a droplight at a hardware store and *safely* hang it in the closet. Next time the closet is painted, ask the painter or paint supplier to add an antimildew agent to the paint. **Note:** Our other advice to your daughter is, don't mix different cleaning products together. It's potentially dangerous, and she's usually not improving upon store-bought versions of the cleaners.

77. Dust for Days

I pride myself at being a pretty good cleaner, but I can't stay ahead of the dust! What am I doing wrong?

Maybe nothing. Some areas and some homes are inherently dustier than others. Here are a few suggestions, though:

1. Even with regular dusting with a feather duster, an occasional thorough dusting with the brush attachment of the vacuum is necessary. Use it on all the things you normally dust, such as molding, windowsills, miniblinds, tables, pictures, and knickknacks. Also use it behind the couch, the TV, and other areas you normally don't vacuum. Change to the furniture attachment, and vacuum the furniture and drapes.

2. Make sure your vacuum isn't spewing the dust back into the room. Change the bag before it is completely full, make sure the fittings and hose are snug, and check to be certain the exhaust isn't clogged. Most vacuums have exhaust filters; if yours does, change it according to the manufacturer's recommendation.

3. Have the carpets professionally cleaned—especially if the dust seems to be the same color as the carpet!

4. Change the filters in your heating and air conditioning systems. Upgrade to improved filters if possible. Or purchase an upgraded type of filtration for your heating, ventilating, and air conditioning system.

5. Prevent dust at its source with doormats in front of every exterior door.

6. Install a portable room air purifier (*HEPA* rated, if allergies are also involved). A purifier can make a big difference. Install it between the probable source of dust (e.g., the front door) and the living area of the room.

7. Eliminate sneaky sources of dust like boxes of pop-up tissues.

8. New carpets can shed a huge amount of fibers at first, so vacuum more often after one has been installed.

9. Caulk around windows and doors, or even replace them in extreme cases.

78.   Cobwebs

I've been having a running battle with cobwebs. Either I'm losing or they're winning. What is the best way to remove cobwebs?

Sometimes one learns more about a subject than one really cares to know. For example, at one time I innocently supposed that all I needed to remove cobwebs was a feather duster. But professional experience has shown me that so many kinds of cobwebs dwell in so many places that no one tool or method will work unfailingly in every circumstance. There are:

1. Cobwebs on ceilings
2. Cobwebs in or on intricate collectibles, plants, chandeliers, et cetera
3. Cobwebs in windows and corners
4. Cobwebs in vents
5. Cobwebs in kitchens, or sticky ones anywhere
6. Cobwebs in the garage, basement, eaves, attic, et cetera

Feather dusters of various sizes will work in some situations. Small flexible feathers work well for delicate items, plants, chandeliers, and so forth. Longer, more rigid feathers are best for cobwebs in vents, corners, and windows. But you'll need a brush to remove sticky cobwebs and maybe even *Red Juice* to remove ones stuck to a wall. If your house has high or rough ceilings, beams, or other areas from which cobwebs are hard to remove, a *ceiling and wall brush* on an extension pole is the answer. An old-fashioned straw broom is just the thing to vanquish an accumulation of many years of cobwebs from the garage or attic or basement. By the way, we're convinced that some spiders spin stickier webs than others and that one or more species must be invisible.

79. Dog Dragging in Dirt

My dog and my husband both keep dragging in dirt and mulch from the garden. I'm particularly fond of the dog, so I'm interested in finding a solution. Any ideas?

We'll tackle the easy part first. Your dog probably has a favorite sleeping spot in the garden somewhere. It's cool and comfortable there. Coax him or her to rest in a cleaner, more civilized outdoor location of your choice by putting a bed in that spot. Or put an old blanket or towel at the place in the garden where the dog sleeps. Two other things you can do: (1) Dedicate one entry for the dog, and *hang* a brush near that door. (Don't just set it near the door. It will disappear before the week is out.) Whoever opens the door to let the dog in should use it to brush off the dirt/mulch mixture before the dog is allowed to enter. (2) Long hair catches mulch, so consider giving the dog a haircut . . . seriously . . . especially if the dog is also uncomfortably warm in hot weather.

You also mentioned your husband as a culprit. Husbands are more resistant to training as well as to brushing. However, the same routine would also work on yours, although the summer haircut won't be as effective. **Note:** I assume you have doormats in place. (See Question 118.) Also, supplement the brush with a towel in wet weather. Use it to wipe the dog's feet before mud is tracked throughout the house.

80. Painted Pet Pig

My husband was painting the fence and our pet pig stepped in the paint can and then ran into the house across our wood floor. Help!

Pet pig, you say? Have you seen *America's Funniest Home Videos*? If you captured the event on tape, it might be worth big bucks!

If the paint was water-based and it's been only a few days or weeks, you will probably be able to get it up by wetting the pig prints with a dilute *ammonia solution* or even dishwashing soap and warm water. This will work especially well if the floor wasn't perfectly clean at the time of the great race. If that was the case, the paint won't have adhered to the floor very well, and the water and cleaning solution should loosen it relatively easily. If you had washed the floor just before the pig's escapade, you might have to coax the paint loose with a plastic *scraper* or *stiff-bristled brush* after applying the solution. Keep the amount of water to a minimum, especially near cracks in the floor or *floor coating*.

Oil-based paint is obviously more of a problem. Ammonia and water will still work if the floor was a bit dirty. If the floor was clean, resort to lighter fluid or mineral spirits and a plastic scraper or *white pad*. You don't have to worry that the *solvent* will remove the floor coating, but pretest to be sure it won't dull the surface. Plan on rewaxing afterward.

81.　Fleas

Is there a cleaning solution to fleas, or must I resort to poisons?

There is a solution. But first you need to understand the life cycle of the flea to understand what must be done. It's somewhat horrific, but as explained to me by my dog's favorite caregiver, San Francisco veterinarian Daniel Hershberger, it goes something like this: Adult fleas are homebodies. Once they're on the host, they prefer to stay there for the balance of their lives.

They don't hop on and off. Flea eggs, however, do fall off the animal. The eggs hatch into larvae, which wriggle to a protected area—e.g., in or under the edge of a carpet. They dine on flea feces that fall in the same area. The larvae turn into cocoons that can remain inactive for months. This hard-cased cocoon stage is so well protected that it's resistant to some pesticides. But when conditions are right—including temperature, moisture, and availability of food (such as a dog or cat . . . or its owner, for that matter)—the cocoon can hatch into a full-size flea in as little as sixty seconds. Discouraging, eh?

The secret, then, to controlling fleas is to vacuum them up when they are in the egg, larval, or cocoon stages of their nasty little lives. This is easy enough to do in theory, but it requires attention and repetition. Flea eggs are about the size of a grain of salt, and the other stages are even bigger, so most vacuums will capture them in their dust bags. But vacuum the carpet slowly enough that the flea eggs, larvae, and cocoons can be pulled up and out of the carpet. Vacuum thoroughly. Go six inches or so under the edge of carpeting, as well as completely under beds and furniture. Either put a chunk of flea collar in your vacuum bag, or remove the dust bag after each vacuuming, seal it (tie it up inside a plastic grocery bag), and discard it. In addition, wash the animal's bedding every few weeks at least.

If you also keep most of the fleas off the animals by regular washing with flea shampoo or with monthly pills (talk to a vet), your home will be essentially flea free with no chemicals at all, except for the shampoo. Can you say "flea free" quickly ten times?

82. Wicker Furniture

You have to look at it closely, but my wicker furniture is really filthy. How should I clean it?

What's difficult about wicker furniture, for cleaning purposes, is that dust settles in out-of-the-way places on the individual strands used to weave the furniture. Use the brush attachment of your vacuum. Better yet, use it along with a handheld *dusting brush.* Loosen the dirt with the dusting brush while holding the vacuum close by to inhale the dislodged dust. **Note:** There are those who swear that putting wicker furniture into the shower once a year removes lots of dirt and is actually good for the furniture: it helps keep it flexible or something. I have my doubts—unless you get in the shower, too, and scrub the furniture with a soft brush and soap—but it may be worth a try. Just don't send us a bill if it all unravels.

83. Body Odor

How do I get body odor out of upholstery?

Have it professionally cleaned. If you're not so inclined, use detergent and water or an upholstery cleaner. Use minimal amounts of cleaner, letting the suds (not water) do the cleaning, and agitate gently with a *cleaning cloth* (occasionally even a *toothbrush*). Blot excess moisture with fresh cleaning cloths. Work in small sections. There may be rental equipment available if you want to go down that path. Good luck. In the future ask your brother-in-law to sit elsewhere.

84. Rolltop Desk

My rolltop desk (not really an heirloom, but it's old enough to be) has collected grunge in the little grooves between the wood slats that do the rolling. How do I get dirt out of there?

Once again the brush attachment of a vacuum cleaner comes in handy. Use it to dig into those grooves and remove all the loose dirt. Clean the remaining dirt out with *Red Juice*–moistened cotton swabs (Q-Tips). If you're still in the mood, a wipe with furniture polish should bring back the shine, and your desk should start to look like the heirloom it may become.

85. Chandeliers

How do I clean chandeliers?

Preparation is the key to resolving many of life's problems, and chandeliers are no exception. But preparation isn't very satisfying because it may not feel as if you're actually doing anything. You're just, well, preparing to do something. That's probably why so little prep work is done. But you must prepare before doing any cleaning, or you could cause more harm than any new cleanliness might compensate for.

First, because the chandelier obviously has to be turned off during this exercise, arrange for alternate lighting, if necessary, so you can see what you're doing. Since we assume you regard the preservation of life and limb as a high priority, we urge you to put a piece of tape over each electrical switch that can electrify the chandelier (and you!) during your cleaning efforts. Perhaps greater than the risk of shock is the risk that you might be startled while perched on the ladder and lose your balance. Who knows what you might grab as you fall? Remember that scene from *Phantom of the Opera* where the chandelier descends with such spectacular results? Need we go on? Actually we will, for the truly prudent will throw the circuit breaker or unscrew the fuse that serves the chandelier. This is the safest way to proceed. However, it will probably complicate providing a source of alternate lighting. (Time to find that extension cord.)

If the chandelier hangs above a table, move the table completely out of the way. Now put a dropcloth, a thick layer of newspapers, towels, or multiple *cleaning cloths* under the chandelier and the surrounding over-spray areas. Use a sturdy ladder or step stool if you need one, and start by removing the lightbulbs because they actually conduct or wick liquid cleaner into the sockets. Clean the bulbs themselves with a *Blue Juice*–dampened cleaning cloth before replacing them.

Use either a solution of clear *ammonia* and water (up to one part ammonia to three parts water) in a spray bottle or a commercial chandelier cleaner in an aerosol or pump form. Liberally spray either solution onto every part of the chandelier that you want to clean, until it is dripping freely onto the towels or what have you below.

Avoid, without being overly paranoid about it, the light sockets. A bit of spray in the sockets shouldn't hurt anything as long as you let them dry thoroughly before you turn on the fixture again. To avoid getting the sockets wet, you can poke a corner of a *cleaning cloth* into empty sockets when spraying around them. Or after spraying, you can blot up any standing solution.

Once you've sprayed the chandelier thoroughly, allow the cleaning solution to drip for a few minutes. Then use a dry cleaning cloth to wipe only the easy-to-reach and visible parts of the chandelier from the top down. Resist the impulse to fuss, and allow the balance of the chandelier to air-dry.

If you noticed any rust while you were up there spraying cleaner all over the place, it would be a good idea to speed up the drying (and slow down the rusting) by turning up the heat or aiming a fan at the chandelier until it's dry.

86. Ceiling Fans

How do you clean ceiling fans?

Forget better mousetraps. What the world really needs is a self-cleaning ceiling fan or, failing that, at least one that you can raise and lower like a flag. As it is, ceiling fans are much too difficult to reach. And when you do, they won't stay still.

If the fan hasn't been cleaned in some time and the blades are as dusty as we suspect, it's best to rise to their level. Trying to clean a very dirty ceiling fan from the floor is exasperating and ineffective. Obviously a ladder is needed in most cases, but once you are there, the cleaning itself is easy enough. Position the ladder once, and then turn the fan blades to clean each one in turn. Use *cleaning cloths* and *Red Juice*. Spray the cloth or the blade (it's easier and safer to spray the cloth), and wipe. Use one cloth to make the first wipe. This cloth will soon be a mess, but it will remove most of the dirt. Use a second Red Juice–dampened cloth for a second and final wipe.

Once you get the fan blades clean, keep them that way with regular

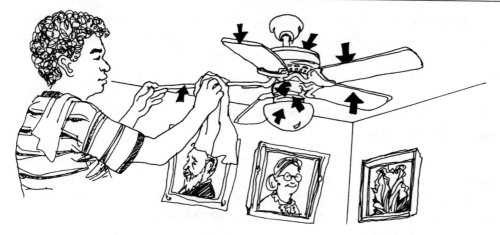

maintenance cleaning. This can be done from the relative safety of terra firma. Use a flexible duster on an extension pole. The one we use is called a *rabbit ear duster*. It has a bendable, double-loop wire frame head (it looks as if it had ears, hence the name) that's covered with a thick 100-percent cotton-yarn head mounted on an extension pole. The tool allows you to clean out-of-reach fans, and you can bend and shape the "ears" to match the contours of the fan. Use the rabbit ear duster dry to remove the bulk of the dirt. If necessary, dampen it with Red Juice, and finish wiping the fan in the same manner.

Note: When installing a new ceiling fan, position it on the ceiling so you can reach it by ladder without having to move heavy furniture. For example, don't place the fan directly over a king-size bed. Install it close enough to the foot of the bed that it will be easily accessible by ladder.

87. Dirty Miniblinds—Are There Any Other Kind?

I have Levolors (miniblinds) in most of the rooms of my house. I've had them for several years and have to admit that I've never touched them when I was housecleaning. I kind of forgot about them. Recently I looked at one up close. They're filthy! How do I clean them?

I have strong opinions about miniblinds that you may want to read eventually. They are set forth directly after this answer, but for reasons that will be clear to you later, you should not read them if you are exceptionally fond of miniblinds. To answer your question, however, there are two general approaches to miniblind cleaning:

1. If the miniblinds are grossly dirty, the first and by far best choice is to look in the yellow pages under "Venetian Blind Cleaners" or "Miniblind Cleaners." You will find quite a number of listings under one of these headings. (That ought to give you a clue to how nasty this job is.) Someone from

one of these companies will race to your home in the morning, whisk your miniblinds away, and then rush them back to you in the afternoon sparkling clean and dry. Most of these companies use an ultrasonic cleaning process—the same type used by jewelers.

2. A distant second choice for very dirty miniblinds is to do it yourself. Be forewarned that cleaning them requires the patience of someone negotiating lasting world peace. There is much more surface area on these blinds than one imagines when innocently contemplating the cleaning thereof. Every square inch on every slat must be carefully washed to remove dirt and usually just as carefully dried to avoid streaks. Just thinking about it gives me the willies.

For the brave of heart there are two methods for hand-cleaning miniblinds.

In-place method. If you have only one or two mini-blinds, consider yourself lucky. You can clean them in place. Cover the adjacent window and window frame with *cleaning cloths* or towels to protect them from overspray. Or you can ignore the overspray and wash them as well. Starting from the top, spray the miniblinds dripping wet with clear *ammonia solution* (up to one part ammonia to three parts water) or chandelier cleaner. Then turn the slats to expose the other side, and spray them again so both sides are dripping wet.

Unless you have very soft water, you must wipe each slat dry to avoid streaks and water spots. Use cleaning cloths to dry them, also working from the top down. When you're finished, raise the miniblinds and clean the frame and then the window behind the blinds. (See Questions 132 and 140.) Then lower the blinds again to air-dry.

Remove-and-clean method.   If you have a number of blinds, it's easier to remove them and make a single big mess elsewhere. The best place—if you have the opportunity and if the weather is accommodating—is outside, mounted against something. It's even better if there is concrete or grass below so you can use the hose without creating a swamp. The perfect spot is in front of the door or the wall of a garage. Use wire or rope temporarily to hang the fully extended blinds. In this case it's easier to put the *ammonia solution* in a bucket and use a *soft-bristled brush* to scrub the blinds rather than spraying them with the cleaning solution. First turn the slats to the down position to scrub them gently. Turn them around, and repeat the process to clean the back side. Now use a hose to rinse, if you can do so without making a muddy mess underfoot. If the water is hard in your area, let the blinds drip for a few minutes, and then wipe each slat dry to avoid spots and streaks. Alternatively, a final rinse by spraying with distilled water will allow you to air-dry the blinds with only minimal spotting. You will also gain quite a reputation in your neighborhood.

If you don't have such a site available, hang the blinds inside the shower, and clean them as described above. Or soak them in the tub. Good luck.

If the blinds are too big to fit into the shower or tub, put them, fully open with slats in the down position, on a flat grassy area. Clean with the same ammonia solution and soft-bristled brush, only now you'll need an extension pole to reach the middle of the blinds. Turn them over, clean the other side, and then rinse with a hose. Move them to another place to dry, or rehang them while still wet and dry them in place. This is not a project you would attempt in Boston in January.

Highly Opinionated Note: Whenever I answer cleaning questions, I know that at least one will be about dirty miniblinds. I try to answer these questions honestly and openly and to be helpful and courteous. But anyone who has ever cleaned house for a living dreads them. Each of the seemingly endless slats is horizontal and therefore catches every particle of passing dust. Then the dust gets wet from ambient moisture and redries as a miniature layer of adobe mud.

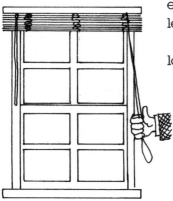

If you don't own any miniblinds now, keep up the good work. Don't be tempted even by half-off sales. Your household cleaning burden will be forever lighter if you resist. **Note:** Vertical blinds don't present the same problems. Consider installing them instead.

For the millions of suffering people who own miniblinds, I offer the following suggestions:

1. Raise the blinds as high as they'll go, and leave them there forever.
2. If you must lower them, turn the slats so they are as close to vertical as possible.
3. Once they are clean, dust them regularly to prevent the adobe phenomenon.
4. Sell them at a garage sale, give them to anyone who will take them, or sell the house.

88.   Clean Miniblinds?!

Okay, smarty-pants, after talking to you on the telephone about my dirty miniblinds (and hating every minute of your answer), I took your advice and had them professionally cleaned. Now that they are clean, what must I do to keep them that way? (I'm sure I won't like this answer, either, but I'm trying to cope.)

I love questions about *clean* things! Keep them as often as possible in their fully raised position, where they can't collect dust. You may think that you shouldn't do that, but if you normally leave them in the lowered position with the slats open, what's the difference? Lower them and turn the slats down when you need privacy or protection from the sun.

Dust miniblinds routinely with a feather duster (see Question 77) or with the brush attachment of a vacuum cleaner. When using a feather duster, use back-and-forth motions, not up-and-down motions, as we discuss in *Speed Cleaning*. If dust starts to build up in spite of regular dusting, wipe the slats with a *cleaning cloth* moistened with *Blue Juice*. It's time consuming but less aggravating than waiting until you have to take them down to clean and less expensive than having them cleaned professionally.

89. Wood Blinds

I have three sets of beautiful wood blinds. I find them very difficult to clean. I have not found many suggestions anywhere. I bought a blind-cleaning gizmo with five woolly "fingers" that just doesn't work. It gets stuck in the blinds and cleans only the middle of the slat, and even that is not thorough. Help! Do you have any ideas?

I have learned that when cleaning products are described by words like *gizmo*, *thingamabob*, *thingamajig*, and *whatchamacallit*, they probably don't work. Better choices are *gimmick, irritation,* and *getyour-moneyback.*

Because of their vulnerability to water, your wood blinds can't be treated like miniblinds. They must be hand-wiped, one slat at a time. Use a *polishing cloth* dampened with furniture polish to wipe each slat. Use so little polish that you don't have to wipe each slat dry also. Streaks aren't as noticeable on wood slats as on the metal or plastic slats of miniblinds, but wipe carefully and thoroughly to avoid having to touch up dirty areas after you think you've finished.

Once you get them clean, follow the instructions for miniblinds and dust them with an ostrich-down feather duster or the vacuum brush attachment. The key is to be consistent about the dusting. You can't just dust when company is coming, because a buildup over time will have to be painstakingly hand-removed. You don't have to dust every square inch of every slat each time you clean, but rotate them and dust some of them each time, or dust all of them in one room each time. As with miniblinds, wood blinds will stay cleaner longer if you leave them in the fully raised position as often as possible and turn the slats down whenever the blinds are in the lowered position.

Chapter 5

FLOORS

90. Which Floor Finish?

Whenever I ask someone a question about the care of my wood floors, I get this question right back: "What are your floors finished with?" If I knew that I wouldn't be asking how to care for them. Duh.

I know it's frustrating, but once you find out, you'll never have to cross that bridge again.

First let's clarify the difference between *floor finish* and *floor coating*. The floor finish is the top protective layer. It's usually a liquid *acrylic* (e.g., The Clean Team High-Gloss Acrylic Floor Finish, Future, et cetera) or paste or liquid wax (e.g., Johnson's paste wax or The Clean Team Fortified Floor Wax). The floor coating is more permanent and lies directly under any floor finish. Examples are polyurethane and varnish. (Polyurethane coatings usually require no floor finish.) (See the illustration on p. 109.)

You are asked that question so often because it's either the finish or the coating that you actually clean—not the wood itself. If you know what the finish is, the usual advice is to continue with the same one. If you know what the coating is, you can get down to business.

The most common coating for the last forty years or so has been polyurethane, a liquid plastic that dries to a beautiful and ferociously durable finish. Your family and guests and dogs and any other critters that occupy your home can practically skate on it with minimal damage. Other potential floor coatings, especially in older homes, are varnish, shellac, or a stain and wax finish called Swedish finish. It's also possible that the floor has no coating on it at all.

There is no easy test to verify what type of coating is on the floor, but you should try to find out. Either: (1) locate the builder and ask, or call in an expert (see "Floor Refinishing" in the yellow pages) and find out once and for all, or (2) err on the side of caution, and follow the directions for polyurethane floors in Question 91.

Whatever the coating, take into account its condition. Does it protect the wood completely, or is it damaged or missing in some areas? Cracks between floorboards, scratches that cut through the coating, and/or well-worn areas in high-traffic zones mean that the wood itself is exposed. This is where it's particularly easy for water to get between and under the wood and cause the hardwood floor or even the subfloor to warp.

If the coating is compromised in areas, use very little cleaning solution—or even none at all—and just vacuum or dust-mop those areas instead. Damaged or worn floors ultimately must be sanded and refinished or replaced.

91. Polyurethane

There are wood floors throughout our new (to us—definitely not new) house. I love the floors, but I have no idea how to take care of them, although they are polyurethane coated according to the real-estate agent. Tell me what to do with all these floors!

Wood floors are probably the most expensive item in a home that you have much control over. Since they are so important to the appearance of your "new" home, it's essential that you know how to maintain and protect this valuable asset. (By the way, we're using *polyurethane, urethane,* and *Varathane* as synonymous terms.)

Maintain the shine of wood floors with regular sweeping, vacuuming, and washing with a mild, no-rinse, no-residue floor cleaner (again, we like clear *ammonia*) but *not* by applying wax or *acrylic floor finish.*

Polyurethane *floor coatings* are quite durable and would maintain their appearance for years were dirt and grime not ground into them by foot traffic. That's why regular, as opposed to sporadic, maintenance is so important. Eventually (exactly how eventual depends on how well the floors are maintained), the floors will show signs of wear and start to lose their shine. The proper response to this is to apply additional coats of polyurethane. As long as no wax, acrylic, or silicone has been applied to the coating, adding coats of polyurethane is a relatively easy job that you can tackle yourself if you're so inclined. It involves renting a rotary floor machine to superclean and slightly abrade the old finish. Then you can apply a new coat or two of polyurethane with an applicator pad.

But if wax, acrylic, or silicone (present in some floor cleaners) has been applied, there is no way to remove these products well enough to allow additional coats of polyurethane to adhere properly. Instead the floor must be sanded back down to the bare wood. This is a *big* job. You'll practically have to move out of house and home. *Everything* you own will be covered with sawdust. *We repeat: If you have polyurethane-coated floors, do not apply wax or acrylic floor finish.*

92. Varnish

Our charming restored Victorian bed-and-breakfast and personal home has original floors with their original floor finish. We've invested a lot of time and money in this project. Tell us how to take care of the floors. (My wife says she will help.)

Varnish was used long before polyurethane, and though it is a beautiful finish, it is not as durable. Traditionally a paste wax (such as Johnson's paste wax) or a liquid *floor wax* (such as our Fortified Floor Wax) has been applied on top of varnish to improve durability and to add shine. Apply additional thin coats of either wax as needed. Keep the floors free of dirt and grime with frequent vacuuming, dust-mopping, and an occasional damp-mopping. Years ago varnish-coated wood floors were not installed in kitchens or bathrooms. If you have finished wood floors in either room, they're practically guaranteed to be polyurethane.

Proper maintenance will drastically increase the length of time between future coats of wax. (See Question 117.) Add as few coats of wax as possible, because the time may come when you'll have to remove them. **Note:** Conventional wisdom is that if a hardwood floor has a heavy wax buildup, then: (1) the floor is old, because wax hasn't been in general use on wood floors since the introduction of Varathane and other plastic coatings; and (2) because it's old, it probably has other problems, such as worn areas, stains, and scratches. Accordingly, most people completely refinish wood floors under these circumstances rather than strip them.

93. Cleaning Wood Floors

I'm afraid to do anything with my hardwood floors, so they're getting dirtier and dirtier. But every time I think about washing them, I get nervous about putting water on them. Can I safely wash them?

Sure. But only the kitchen and bathroom floors need regular washing. In other rooms, just dust-mop and vacuum. As you suspect, the greatest danger when you wash wood floors comes from the water rather than the cleaning agent. Be sparing with the amount of water you use—especially if the *floor coating* is damaged at all. (Even if you can't see damage, there are often small cracks in the coating, especially between the floorboards, that can allow water to seep down to where it can cause serious mischief.) (See Question 96.) Don't put water or cleaning solution directly on the floor. Don't use a "dripping wet" mop. Wring it out so that it is only "almost dripping wet" and work in one small section at a time. A dilute clear *ammonia solution* is one of the safest cleaners available.

94.　Cleaning Wood Floors with Plain Water

I can't figure out how to clean my wood floors that have been coated with polyurethane. Right now I'm washing them with plain water, as recommended by the installer, but they never seem to be completely clean. Help!

The only reason a manufacturer would recommend plain water is to limit exposure to product-liability lawsuits. It's a litigious world out there. But plain water is a particularly cruel solution because it just doesn't get floors clean! Polyurethane is one of the most durable coatings on the planet, so it's perfectly safe to use a mild solution of almost any floor cleaner (e.g., clear *ammonia)* and water. As discussed in the previous question, the water is probably more dangerous than the cleaning agent to a wood floor.

95.　Stripping Wood Floors

Can I strip hardwood floors?

No. It's not safe to strip wax from wood floors using conventional methods (water and stripper) because the amount of chemicals and water required will probably cause severe damage to the floor and subfloor. Try cleaning or buffing the floors to help their appearance. The only other alternatives are dry-cleaning stripping methods that require professional assistance, or sanding and refinishing the floors.

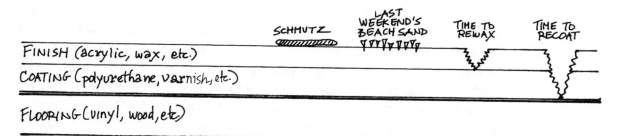

96. Water Stain on Floor

I bought my husband a ficus plant for his birthday and dutifully slid a saucer under it to protect the zillion-dollar new hardwood floor we just had installed. Well, I moved it the other day and discovered, to my horror, that a huge ring has appeared beneath it. My husband hasn't spotted it yet. I need an answer and I need it *now*.

You sure do. As the expression goes, time is of the essence. Sounds as if you used a terra-cotta saucer, which, as you know by now, does a dandy job of transmitting moisture from the plant to the floor. You'd better replace it with a plastic, glass, or other impermeable saucer ASAP, but you have more pressing matters to attend to.

Edward S. Korczak of the National Wood Flooring Association has probably come to your rescue. He recommends applying Zud plus enough water to make a paste or poultice (the consistency of toothpaste). Smear a quarter-inch layer of paste on the ring, let it dry to a powder, utter a few incantations, and vacuum the powder away when it is thoroughly dry. Pretest a dime-size area first. Unless you've led a charmed life, you will have to repeat this procedure. Maybe you should suggest to your startled husband that it's a good time to go on a weekend fishing trip or bowling tour with his buddies.

97.   Vinyl Floors:
Using the Manufacturer's Cleaner

The manufacturer of my kitchen's vinyl flooring told me to use only his cleaners. Is he right?

I suppose we can't blame him for trying to earn a living. But it's your floor now, and you can clean it with practically any reputable cleaning product in the world, without damaging it and without the permission of the manufacturer.

98.   Cleaning Vinyl with Vinegar and Water

I've got an Armstrong Solarian floor in my kitchen. I'm worried that strong floor cleaners could destroy the finish. I've tried hot water with disinfectant and vinegar, but this doesn't do a great job, and frankly, it smells funny. What would you use?

Funny? I imagine it smells downright peculiar. I recommend a dilute clear *ammonia solution*. It smells, too, but not quite as funny.

Vinegar is the weakest of acids. By the time it's further diluted in water, its effectiveness as a cleaner is virtually nonexistent. You would have about as much luck wishing the floor clean. And don't worry about disinfecting the floor unless you actually do eat off it. Who knows what happens to the effectiveness of the disinfectant when it's mixed with vinegar, anyway? You've heard this before, probably for safety reasons, but you're usually asking for trouble by mixing cleaners. (See Question 94 for floor cleaner suggestions.)

99. Skid Marks

My son likes to do wheelies with his wheelchair in the kitchen. How do I remove the tire skid marks from my vinyl floors?

A thin oil *solvent*, like plain lighter fluid or *De-Zov-All*, is a good starting point. Wipe on the solvent with an old *cleaning cloth* or a paper towel. A *white pad* or steel wool will boost the effectiveness of the solvent impressively. Even an *eraser* (by itself) will work sometimes.

If one of these procedures works up to a point but misses a portion of the tire marks, the wheels may have made indentations or grooves in the floor. In this case switch to a *toothbrush* (plus solvent) to remove the deeper marks. **Discouraging Thoughts:** Wheel rims may have damaged the floor in a way that prevents the marks from being completely removed. Also, solvents do a great job of removing any floor wax along with the tire marks, so you will probably have to rewax the area.

100. Black Heel Marks

I try my best to keep my kitchen floors free of back heel marks, but they keep appearing. It's almost as if little fairies in black-heeled pumps come in the night and dance on my floor. What's the solution?

Do they leave pixie dust too? Proceed with caution, as fairies have a wicked sense of humor.

If you're lucky, a simple gum *eraser* may remove the heel marks. It's personally and environmentally safe and practically free. If it works, leave a couple in a kitchen drawer just for that purpose.

It's just as likely, however, that you'll need a *solvent*. *De-Zov-All* and lighter fluid work well. Apply either to a paper towel or old *cleaning cloth* and wipe off the spot. Spray the same area with *Red Juice*, and wipe it with a cleaning cloth to remove all traces of the solvent. Or wash the floor with a detergent floor cleaner when you're finished. Some floors allow marks to come up easily with Red Juice and a *white pad*. You may have to rewax the area you've worked on, and thus the dancing fairies will have had their revenge.

101. Cleaning Nooks and Crannies

I have a vinyl floor with lots of nooks and crannies that look dirty even right after I've cleaned the floor. What's wrong?

Two possibilities come to mind:

1. Mops tend to glide over the top of dirt trapped in the textured areas and grout lines of floors. To dislodge this dirt, occasionally you'll have to clean the floor with a *brush* that can reach down into these hard-to-get-at nooks, crannies, and grout lines. Use clear *ammonia* and water as a cleaning solution. A *wet vacuum* comes in handy to remove the dirty liquid afterward. Remember, this is an occasional job. Mop regularly, and use the brush only when the dirt in the grout lines builds up again.

2. Dirt could be encased in a coat of *acrylic*. (Oh, lucky you.) You can see the dirt through the acrylic, but your cleaner can't get at it. Alas, the solution in this case is to strip the acrylic from the floor and reapply a new acrylic finish.

102. Stripping a Vinyl Floor

How do I go about stripping a vinyl floor?

Sorry, it would take more room than this book can spare to answer your question properly. This is probably the most difficult single housecleaning job, especially if the wax is old and built up in many glasslike layers. Luckily, *Spring Cleaning* has an utterly fascinating chapter devoted entirely to this ordeal. Available at bookstores throughout the globe.

103. Waxing No-Wax Floors

I have a no-wax floor in my kitchen. Every time I look at it, I think I should be waxing it or doing *something* with it. Should I wax a no-wax floor?

Usually not. That was the whole idea in the first place. But this is the most commonly asked question about no-wax floors. A quality vinyl floor, even with average maintenance, will last for years and years. Sadly, the converse is true: some inexpensive ones never look great—even with the addition of wax. Once you start waxing, it's a never-ending process of reapplying more wax, stripping it, and then waxing again. It's incalculably easier to protect the floor through routine maintenance. However, you may think that the floor needs or deserves the protection of an additional finish because of the amount of dirt that's tracked into your home or because you don't mop or vacuum as often as you'd prefer. If so, go right ahead and wax away. Treat it like a regular vinyl floor and use a liquid finish such as The Clean Team's High-Gloss *Acrylic Floor Finish*. The technique is described in Question 106.

104.   Stripping No-Wax Floors

Can I strip and rewax a no-wax floor?

Sure! As long as there's a serious enough buildup of wax or *acrylic*. It's difficult to tell sometimes, because dirt on the floor can look like wax in need of stripping. Scrub an area well to be sure. If it comes clean, then it doesn't have to be stripped. It just needs a good cleaning.

105.   How Often?

How often should I strip and rewax a vinyl kitchen floor?

It's more of a judgment call than a calendar event. It depends on: (1) the amount of foot (including paw) traffic; (2) how often you regularly wash and vacuum or sweep the floor (have you noticed how often that word *regularly* keeps popping up in these answers about floor care?); (3) the age of the floor (new floors hold their shine longer than old ones); (4) how many coats of *acrylic floor finish* are already on the floor; and (5) your fondness for shiny floors. When it doesn't look satisfactory to you even after washing or applying more acrylic finish, it's time to strip off the old coats and start anew.

106.   How to Wax

How do I wax my kitchen floors? I'm not sure what they are, but they're not wood. It's linoleum or something like that.

You should read the previous questions and answers on the subject to be sure you want to start waxing. If so, follow these four steps:

1.   Wash the floor well.

2.   Strip old wax from the floor (if necessary).

3.   Apply two or three very thin, very even coats of *floor sealer* using a fake-wool wax applicator. The cheapest and the most expensive applicators yield comparable results. Allow each coat to dry before applying the next coat. It's dry when it's no longer sticky to the touch. Try not to imagine that it's drier than it actually is. (A fan can speed up drying quite a bit.) You can skip a sealer and your floor will still be protected by the *acrylic floor finish* (to be applied next), but the floor may be a bit less shiny and the finish less durable.

4. Apply two or three very thin, very even coats of liquid acrylic floor finish. Use the same applicator that you used for the sealer (if any), likewise allowing each coat to dry before proceeding.

107. Wax Traffic Areas Only

Can I get away with rewaxing only the part of the floor that gets heavy traffic? I know I'll feel guilty if I do.

Rewaxing only the traffic areas is absolutely the correct way to do it. So you can skip the guilt. When you apply wax or *acrylic* to the floor, it will stay there until the end of the world or until it is worn off by foot traffic or you strip it off. It doesn't evaporate or disappear by any other means. Accordingly, whenever you add additional coats of wax to areas where no one walks, you're adding layer after layer of unnecessary wax to the floor. All that wax is unnecessary because the original wax is still there and it's all going to have to be stripped off sooner or later—which is a big job. So rewax the entire floor only the first time after stripping it. Don't rewax close to walls or other low-traffic areas on top of previous coats of wax.

108.   Cleaning Waxed Floors

What should I use to clean my waxed floors?

A mild cleaner is necessary so you won't dull the wax finish. Almost any reputable floor-cleaning product will do. Because they save time, we like liquid floor cleaners that don't require rinsing. That eliminates Spic and Span, for example. Clear *ammonia* is a no-rinse type of cleaner and has long been a favorite of ours. But be careful. Too strong a solution of ammonia will damage the existing wax coat. Ammonia in sufficient proportions is actually a superb wax stripper! It's a balancing act: use an *ammonia solution* that's strong enough to dislodge the dirt but weak enough to avoid demolishing the finish. Test a couple of different dilutions to find one that works for your floor's particular combination of wax and dirt. Dirt dulls wax quickly, so keep the floors free of dirt and grime with regular attention, using a good dust mop, a vacuum, or a damp mop between floor cleanings.

109.   Sealing Floors

Should I use a floor sealer to smooth over a textured floor?

No. *Sealers* contain levelers that fill in only microscopic imperfections in the floor. Sealers don't level floors in the sense of filling up visible nooks and crannies in textured floors or grout lines, even though they may make a noticeable overall difference in the level of shine achieved in a textured floor. But a sealer such as *Floor Sealer* can make a *big* difference in the ultimate shininess of smooth floors. It can also improve the general appearance of the floor and help protect it. If you apply *acrylic* to a floor, we recommend that you precede it with several coats of sealer. Apply it with the same fake-wool applicator, and with the same two or three very even, very thin coats. Follow with only one or two coats of acrylic.

110. Adios, Mop & Glo

How do I remove Mop & Glo?

It usually comes off rather easily with a moderate or strong clear *ammonia solution*. We no longer use such products (Mop & Glo, Brite, et cetera) for no-wax flooring because they tend to build up a layer of *acrylic* over time. And it's nearly impossible to wash a floor and simultaneously leave a clean and shiny surface as such products claim to do.

111. Dirty Again Too Quickly

I stripped my floor with an Armstrong product and then I used your Clean Team Sealer and High-Gloss Acrylic Floor Finish. It looked great for a

month, and then it started looking like it had a filmy buildup again. What can I do?

I believe your floor is showing the effects of incorrect mopping. Not enough of the dirt is being removed during mopping, and the remaining dirt is being smeared together to form a film on the floor. It's not visible right away, but over time it becomes apparent. If one is daydreaming about Caribbean cruises or romantic Hawaiian sunsets while mopping, occasionally this happens. Not to worry; here's what to do when mopping: (1) Go over each area as many times as necessary to clean it, not just to get it wet. (2) Make more trips back to the sink to rinse dirt off the mop. (3) Give extra attention to high-traffic areas such as in front of the sink, refrigerator, and stove. When you do, the filmy buildup will disappear. With only a bit of practice you can resume vicarious vacations as you mop. **Note:** Using too rich a cleaning solution can make the floor sticky. We've noticed this regularly with a particular oil soap. Be sure to follow the recommended dilution ratios.

112.   Wet Versus Damp Mopping

When I hear the word *mop*, I guess I know what it means. I get confused, though, when it calls for wet mopping versus damp mopping. What's the diff?

Wet mopping is synonymous with *mopping*. It means cleaning floors with some type of floor cleaner and water, and it's usually the technique of choice for kitchen and bathroom floors. *Damp mopping* is a term reserved for wiping dust from otherwise clean floors with a barely damp mop or cloth and no floor cleaner. Usually this task is reserved for wood floors or floors that aren't exposed to much traffic or grease or other spills. Examples are the floors around the edge of a rug or bedroom floors.

113. Cleaning Marble Floors

How do I clean marble floors?

For starters, a specialized marble cleaner isn't necessary. Almost any reputable floor cleaner will do. As usual, though, it's a good idea to test your choice before you start slopping it all over the place. Very highly polished marble floors show off their scratches like glass. As with any floor, it's the grit and grime caught between the floor itself and shoes that cause scratches. Scratches can be avoided only with regular care.

Marble's other weakness is acids, so don't clean with a *vinegar-and-water* solution, for example. Even the mild acids in citrus drinks, wine, or colas can etch marble, so wipe up and rinse such spills ASAP. As you may know by now, we prefer a dilute *ammonia solu-*

tion as a floor cleaner, and that is what we recommend for marble floors. **Note:** When we suggest that you don't need a specialized marble floor cleaner (or lampshade duster, or a wicker chair cleaner, or whatever), it doesn't mean that you can't—or shouldn't—run right out and purchase a specialty cleaner or that you won't be perfectly thrilled with the results. Our approach is that it's simpler to purchase, store, and follow the directions of only one product for many cleaning jobs rather than have a different cleaner for each.

114.   Shining Marble Floors

How do I shine marble floors?

The most common method of shining is to buff with a rotary floor machine. (If you don't have one sitting in your closet, it can be rented from an equipment rental store.) There are *marble polishes* designed for small floors, such as foyers, that can be buffed by hand. The Premium Marble Polish we use can be buffed by either method. I would call a professional for larger floors because of the amount of heavy labor involved. Marble floors start off shiny. You can keep them that way with careful maintenance. **Note:** *Acrylic floor finishes* are usually a disaster for marble floors.

115.   Terra-Cotta Clay Pavers

The Mexican tiles on my kitchen floor have had some kind of mystery finish applied. Spots have appeared where the finish has been scratched off. I have tried acrylic stripper, but it didn't work. I have also applied *acrylic wax*, but it doesn't cover the spots or make the floor uniform. I guess I have to remove the finish and start fresh.

Maybe not. The floor was probably sealed, and many *sealers* are semipermanent. They're more like paint than wax. Once they dry, they can't be removed using methods designed for removing other floor sealers. So the best solution is to reapply the sealer over the entire floor after you've stripped off any existing wax.

Talk to the manufacturer or installer to find out what sealer was used. If you're unsuccessful, we'll assume a semipermanent sealer was used on the tile because acrylic stripper had no effect. Most tile stores sell this type of sealer, so you can add coat(s) to cover the areas where the sealer has been scratched off.

If these efforts don't work, you'll have to use a professional stripping solution to remove the sealer. This type of stripper involves heavy-duty *solvents*, so you're well advised to hire a professional stripper (hmm . . . this could be fun) to do the work for you.

116. Concrete Floors

What can I do to improve the appearance of my concrete floor?

Start by sweeping or vacuuming followed by a good scrubbing with a moderate *ammonia solution* plus a *brush* or a mop. Add ammonia if more cleaning power is needed. Then rinse thoroughly. A *wet vacuum* makes this part of the job immensely easier. To improve the appearance of a well-finished smooth concrete floor, apply two or three thin coats of *floor sealer* next. Then apply either an *acrylic floor finish* or a traditional paste wax. Concrete is porous enough that several coats of either finish are required. There are new polyurethane tints designed especially for concrete. Painting after cleaning is also an option, but you're better off using a specialized paint. Talk to a paint supplier.

117. Maintaining Floors

What's the best way to maintain my floors?

The Johnson wax folks (who, one supposes, should know a bit about the subject) say there are three rules for floor care:

1. Vacuum them.
2. Vacuum them.
3. Vacuum them.

Evidently they think it's important to keep loose dirt off the floor. We agree. You didn't mention what kind of floor, but the advice applies to every type of floor we're aware of. *Floor finishes* don't lose their shine just from people walking on them. As we've said before, it's the dirt that's caught between the *floor coating* or floor finish and people's shoes that causes most of the real damage. (This is equally true of carpeted floors.)

The best thing you can do for floors is regularly to vacuum, sweep, dust-mop, wash, clean, or do whatever it takes to keep grit and dirt off the floors before they mar the surface.

118. Protecting Floors

How can I extend the life of my floors?

Doormats dramatically reduce the amount of dirt brought into your home, the same dirt and grime that are the primary cause of wear on your floors. Reduce the volume of imported dirt by up to 85 percent by placing mats both inside and outside all entry doors in your home. Install mats that are at least two by three feet and even larger if you can stand it. Coco mats and other grass mats are ineffective because they shed and because it's fiendishly difficult to get accumulated dirt and grit out of them. Use real mats with carpeting over rubber, not carpet remnants whose abrasive backing can scratch floors or create worn spots on the carpet underneath.

Remnants also look dirty all the time and very seldom have clean unraveled edges or edges that will stay flat.

Once you have the mats in place, *vacuum or sweep them regularly*—at least as often as you do the surrounding floors—so they don't become saturated with dirt and lose their effectiveness. Mats—plus regular vacuuming, sweeping, dust mopping, and wet mopping—will mean your floors will last so much longer that you'll get tired of them before they wear out. Better yet, it means that your house will retain its value and will look better during that time.

Chapter 6

CARPETS

In this chapter we'll answer questions about some common carpet accidents plus other carpet-related problems. For the most part, we're talking about *fresh* accidents: the stain hasn't dried, which would have made it immensely more difficult or impossible to remove. If you treat such spills while they're fresh, nearly all stains can be avoided. You may notice that our answers to several questions are similar. That's because the solution is generally the same: Get whatever it is back out of the carpet! For dried stains or for stains we don't mention, there are good books available on the subject (e.g., *How to Remove Spots and Stains* by Professor Herb Barndt [New York: Perigee Books]). If you want to have a go at dried stains, rehydrate (remoisten) the area slightly, and then proceed as if it were a fresh spot. Considering the value of a carpet, if your efforts are unsuccessful or if you're unsure of how to proceed, don't hesitate to call in a professional carpet-cleaning company right away.

119. Red Wine Spills

I've read so many conflicting reports about red wine and carpets: Pour white wine on the red wine, douse it with talcum powder or salt, make a thick paste of borax and water (I don't even know what borax is!), pour on soda water . . . I'm completely at sea. Not that there is any red wine on my carpet at the moment, but when that exciting moment does arrive, what exactly should I do?

Long ago, when I was still a team leader on *The Clean Team*, I was vacuuming a wealthy customer's home. The cord became stuck, so I yanked on it (something I tell team members *never* to do). As fate would have it, the cord was tangled in the legs of a small table holding a crystal decanter of well-aged ruby port. When I yanked the vacuum cord, it upset the table, and the decanter promptly obeyed the laws of gravity. All this happened very quietly because the customer had very thick, very plush, very *white* wool carpeting. Both the sound of that wine (ever so muffled) and the sight of that wine (a sickening blood-red) are forever etched into my memory. It quickly ran through my mind what it might cost to replace the carpeting, and that was enough to move me to immediate action.

Here's what I've learned about such spills: Immediately blot up as much of the wine as possible. Use *cleaning cloths* or towels. Don't waste time looking for old towels. Use your best ones if that's all that's handy. Keep using

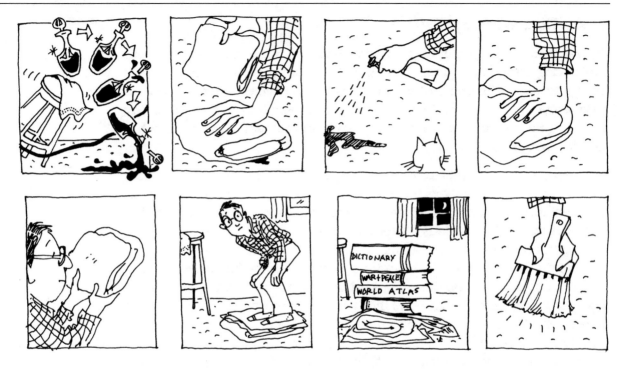

fresh cloths or towels. After you've blotted up as much as you can, spray the area with *Red* or *Blue Juice* or even plain water to remoisten (not re-soak) the area, and blot again. As needed, gently use a *toothbrush* or turn the cloth as you blot to help loosen the last remains of the stain. Remoisten and reblot two or three times until what you're blotting up is colorless or the faint color of Red or Blue Juice, but definitely not the color of wine. Stand on the cloths the last couple of times you blot to apply extra pressure. When finished, place additional layers of clean cloths over the damp area, cover them with several layers of newspapers, and then weigh them down with a few books. Leave overnight. After you remove the books, gently brush or vacuum the nap to match the rest of the carpet.

When I was at that customer's home, I could leave the books only until we'd finished the rest of the cleaning and vacuuming. But that was enough. Even though I had to confess what had happened (after all, the wine was missing), a stain never appeared. **Note:** A good *wet/dry vacuum* will pick up 80 to 90 percent of the wine if you use it promptly. Then switch to cleaning cloths or towels and proceed as above.

Some of the things you read about carpet stains probably work, but some can make things worse, like adding so much liquid to the spill that it soaks the pad or even the floor under the carpet. It might be okay to apply salt or talcum or a similar absorbent to soak up the wine, but you won't know if it worked or not until it dries. Besides, you're more likely to run out of those items than towels. We prefer to take ten minutes or so to solve the problem immediately and be done with it.

120. Traffic Areas Dirty

Okay, Guru of Grunge, here's a problem I'll bet you can't help me with. I have carpeting throughout my house. Unfortunately it's a rather light Berber carpet, so it shows dirt much more easily than I thought when it was installed. That's "a" problem, but it's not "the" problem, which is that the carpeting gets dirty only in traffic areas. The worst is not even at the front door, where I have mats; it's the first few feet into the bedroom and the first few feet into the guest bathroom. It irks me to pay for a professional carpet cleaning when only two small areas are dirty. I guess I'll just have to hire someone, right?

Nope, there is an alternative. Lightly spray *Red Juice* on an area of two square feet or so. Don't overspray. You want an even mist of Red Juice—kind of like morning dew. Then rub that area with a dry but crumpled-up *cleaning cloth.* Just hold it in your fist, and rub it back and forth across the misted area. Turn it often. The cloth will pick up the moisture from the carpet, along with the surface dirt that was annoying you. Change cleaning cloths often, and repeat the process until you've cleaned the dirty area. Toss them into the laundry when you're done. Treat yourself to something fun with the money you've saved! **Note:** We live in an area with red soil that gets on everything and drives everyone crazy. A woman I know took a handful of the dirt with her when she went shopping for new carpeting. She exactly matched her carpet to the dirt. It worked brilliantly.

121. Shoe Polish

How do you remove shoe polish stains from carpeting?

If any solid bits of shoe polish remain, don't try to pick them up or to remove them with a spatula or *scraper*. This will only spread them or rub them in. Get the vacuum, and put the end of the hose over the bits and suck them away cleanly. The next step is to dissolve the remaining polish with a *solvent* like *De-Zov-All* or lighter fluid. Before you try any solvent directly on the shoe polish, test in an *inconspicuous place* to make sure the solvent doesn't damage the carpet fibers. The tricky part is to get the dissolved polish back out of the carpet. Apply a small amount of solvent to the spot, and immediately blot with a *cleaning cloth*. Don't rub. Blot. Repeat as needed. Agitate gently with a *toothbrush* if necessary. When there seems to be nothing left, we like to spray with *Red Juice* one last time and blot again to remove any traces of solvent and polish. As a last step, brush the wet carpet fibers to match surrounding nap.

122. Blood

How do I remove bloodstains from the carpet?

Especially in the case of blood, you have a much better chance when the stain is fresh, so this is no time to stop and mix yourself a drink, much as you may be inclined. Instead thoroughly blot the bloodstained area with a *cleaning cloth* or towel. Blotting (not rubbing) helps avoid spreading the stain. Keep at this until you can't remove any more blood. Lightly rewet several times with *Red Juice* or cool water to dilute the remaining blood, and reblot. If the blood was partially dried, or if there is any stain remaining at this point, rewet with a moderate *ammonia solution*, and gently agitate with a *toothbrush*. Blot, rewet, and reblot. Finally, cover with several layers of cleaning cloths, several layers of newspapers, and books to provide some weight to encourage complete absorption. **Note:** Any remaining bloodstains usually respond well to hydrogen peroxide. Use the milder solution sold for antiseptic purposes, without diluting it further, but you must pretest because hydrogen peroxide is a type of bleach. Rewet, reblot, and cover with cleaning cloths and books as above.

123. Pet Urine

I didn't gain a husband so much as a menagerie. One big dog and two cats. All of which have had occasional wet "mishaps" on the carpets. I've never had this problem before. Help, please.

The secret to the successful removal of urine stains is an abundant supply of both patience and paper towels. A common mistake is to grab a few paper towels, blot up the urine, and call it a day. It looks so much better that we're inclined to think we're finished. Oh, but we're not. There's still more than enough urine left behind to reappear as a stain, and an odor will not be far behind.

Blotting up the urine is only the first step. Until the problem is solved, never run out of paper towels. When your pet has a mishap, use a handful of paper towels to blot up as much moisture as you can. Do this several times. Use plenty of paper towels, and stand on them to blot up as much as possible. The next step, which may seem a bit odd since you've just removed most of the liquid from the carpet, is to spray the area with *Red Juice*—enough to rewet the area with a heavy mist—and blot it up again with fresh paper towels. Urine still remains in the carpet, and the only way to get it out is to dilute the stain and blot it out. Rewet and blot it at least twice. As a last step, place fresh paper towels over the spot, cover them with several layers of newspaper, add a few books for weight, and leave overnight.

If the urine has dried before you discover it, rehydrate the area by spraying with water and blot with paper towels to remove as much of the urine as you can. Do this several times. Now use a specialized stain- and odor-removing *enzyme cleaner* like Pet "OOPS" Remover on the spot. Enzyme products combat stains caused by organic sources: blood, urine, feces, food, grass, and so forth. Protein molecules in the enzyme solution eat the organic ingredients of the stain and then expire (presumably painlessly, but certainly quietly) when their food source—urine in this case—is exhausted. For this reason some enzyme solutions must be mixed fresh to become activated and, once mixed, are good only for a day or two before the protein molecules die of old age, or hunger, or whatever. Enzyme treatments are not instantaneous and may even have to be repeated once or twice, but they work amazingly well and they are quite safe—both to you and to the surface involved. **Note:** There are a number of books on animal behavior that may interest you. Your vet could recommend one, but grown pets shouldn't have this kind of accident in the home.

124. Animal Feces

I have a kitten, and so far I have been doing pretty well cleaning up after her. Let me see, how do I put this? Recently she's had a bout of diarrhea and I'm not doing nearly as well. Advice?

Remove as much of the feces as you can before you start any other cleaning efforts. The best tools are a spatula and a piece of cardboard. Use the spatula to get under the mess, and use the cardboard to stop the spatula at the edge of the mess so you don't spread it. Empty the spatula onto newspapers. Take your time with the spatula, and remove as much as you possibly can before you start the next step.

Spray with *Red Juice* and wipe with paper towels. At first, spray and wipe and respray and rewipe to remove solids instead of rubbing them further into the carpet. When most of the solids are removed, spray with Red Juice, gently agitate with a *toothbrush,* and blot until the spot is gone. Finally, cover the area with *cleaning cloths,* then newspapers, then books for weight, and allow to sit overnight. Residual stains or odors can be treated with an *enzyme cleaner* as in Question 123. **Note:** If the feces are completely dry, lift them off either with a paper towel or with the spatula. Then use the vacuum—either with the crevice tool or the hose with no attachment—to break loose dry particles sticking to the carpet. It will remove practically all of them. Then start with the Red Juice and toothbrush.

125. Grease

A hot and very greasy hamburger patty fell onto my carpet (new, light colored, right in the middle of it) and then got stepped on full force by a 195-pound teenager. How can I get rid of this horrific stain? And thank you for not asking for details about how it happened.

Visions of a "hot potato" game gone horribly wrong keep popping into my mind. This stain is a combination of grease and blood. *Red Juice* is a degreaser and as such would be effective. Spray the stain with Red Juice, gently agitate with a *toothbrush,* and then blot thoroughly with a *cleaning cloth.* It's a good idea to fold the cloth and put it over the stain, and then stand on the cloth for a few seconds. Do this several times: spray, agitate, blot, spray, and so on. After you have blotted for the last time, place additional dry cloths, a few newspapers, and then several heavy books over the stain. Leave them there overnight. This last step is important and unfortunately is sometimes skipped because it looks as if the stain has been completely removed. However, as the carpet dries, moisture evaporating from the carpet fibers "pulls" more stain material up from deep in the carpet. This will cause the stain to reappear, much to your horror, the next day. Avoid that by repeated wetting and blotting *and* by placing weighted absorbent material over the stain overnight. If there are residual bloodstains, use an *ammonia solution* as in Question 122.

126.   Tape Residue

How do I get tape off my carpet?

A *solvent* is required to remove the gummy residue. *De-Zov-All,* lighter fluid, lacquer thinner, or nail-polish remover are all potential candidates. Some laundry pretreatments will also work. Use the same techniques as used for removing shoe polish in Question 121.

127.   Gum

How do I get chewing gum out of a carpet?

The usual advice from professionals is to freeze the gum, whack it with the back of a spoon, and remove the shattered remains. Unfortunately, the method available to most consumers to freeze the gum is an ice cube, and I haven't seen ice work all that well in my lifetime—but then again I haven't gone completely gray.

Much also depends upon the disposition of the gum. Here is our advice:

1.   **If the gum is sitting on the surface of the carpet.** Stalk up to it, grab it with your bare hands, and yank. It just might come loose, if you've led a charmed and virtuous life. If not, the freeze-and-whack technique is next on the agenda. The idea is to chill the gum to the point that it becomes brit-

tle. Many of the mishaps involved with an ice cube probably stem from not taking the time to lower the temperature enough so the gum gets brittle in its full thickness. If your fingers turn blue, use ice tongs to hold the cube. **Note:** A commercial aerosol freezing agent will increase your chances of success immeasurably. It's available at janitorial supply stores and some carpet stores.

You're not quite ready to whack yet. When you bring down the spoon, it may shatter the glob into little bits of gum that scatter everywhere. Position a piece of paper or cardboard over the gum with a hole cut out of the middle, or have a vacuum cleaner standing by with the crevice attachment to nab little bits before they warm up and reattach themselves wherever they fall.

Once the gum is thoroughly brittle, you can do the traditional whack with the back of a big spoon or you can try to gingerly pry off the gum with a spatula. In either case traces of gum will probably hold on for dear life, so finish up with a swipe or two using a cloth dipped in a *solvent* like *De-Zov-All*, lighter fluid, or lacquer thinner. (Pretest, pretest, pretest.) Then feel the area with your hand. If it feels sticky in the slightest way (no cheating!), you're not finished. Resume swiping. When it's finally clean to the touch, give the area a final spray with *Red Juice*, and blot dry. A nice finishing touch is to reset the nap of the carpet by brushing lightly with the *toothbrush*.

If freeze-and-whack didn't work, cut under the gum with a pair of scissors to remove it.

2. If the gum is smooshed into the body of the carpet. Cut out part of it if you can do so without shortening the carpet fibers so much that it will be noticeable afterward. Use *De-Zov-All* or other solvent to dissolve the gum and a *cleaning cloth* to blot it up. According to Frank Gromm III, the carpet expert from Montara, California, even stubborn cases will eventually capitulate to lacquer thinner if you're patient. Keep working toward the middle of the gum so you don't spread it even further. A spatula will usually help your efforts along.

And we hope the person who did the chewing in the first place will have the pleasure of trying to remove the gum—or at least of watching you so he or she can remove the wad the next time.

128. Bleach on Carpet

Like an idiot I managed to leave a trail of drops of bleach all the way from the kitchen to the bathroom. Our beautiful beige carpet now has about fifty little white spots on it. Is there anything that can be done?

Sorry to hear your carpet has a crop of reverse freckles. But you're not an idiot. It can happen to anyone. The bad news is that bleach permanently removes color. It's G-O-N-E gone. The good news is that you'll probably be able to replace the color so well that you'll scarcely notice. Well, *you may* notice, but nobody else will.

As for the source of the replacement colors, you have several choices. Probably the best is an artist's felt-tip pen. A good artist's supply store will have an amazing assortment of several hundred colors available. Three brand names are Prismacolor, AdMarker, and Chartpak. The hardest part is trying to decide which color(s) to select. If you have a carpet remnant, bring it to the store. Watercolor paints also work and help you avoid a trip to a store if you have them at hand, but they are somewhat more time consuming.

To restore the color, the strategy is to err on the side of a color lighter than the surrounding unbleached carpet. Also, it's best to dab on the colors in small dots. Your eye can be tricked by a few dots of color more easily than by a solid blob, so "less is better" definitely applies in this case. You'll probably find that a combination of two or three colors will fool your eye better than a single one. This is especially true if the carpet is a blend of colors itself. Whatever method you choose, go easy. Practice on a remnant if you can locate one. On the real thing, start with the most inconspicuous spot, even though your impulse will be to tackle the most obvious one first.

Bear in mind that unless you use permanent aniline-dye marking pens, these repairs are profoundly temporary. They will fade in sunlight—maybe even moonlight—and will go away when you shampoo the carpet. Think of it as carpet cosmetics. **Note:** If this whole project gives you the jitters, call in a professional in a heartbeat.

129. Burned Spots

How do you fix a burned spot on a carpet?

The solution is to get rid of the burned ends of the carpet fibers. There are two ways to do this. In the order in which you should try them: (1) Use a piece of fine sandpaper to sand off the burned ends. (2) Cut them away with a straight-edge razor in a holder, if you can do so without cutting your finger, or use scissors if you can't be trusted with the razor blade. Use a pair of tweezers to hold up each burned carpet fiber and then cut as close to the burn as you can.

Once you've done this, either you have slightly shorter fibers that no one will ever notice, or the fibers are so short that the carpet backing is visible. If the latter is the case, one solution is to cut some fibers from a remnant or a hidden area of the carpet (e.g., under a piece of furniture or in the corner of a closet). Glue the transplanted fibers into the area where fibers were cut out. (Anything from Elmer's or another clear-drying glue all the

way to the amazing five-minute epoxies will do.) It's possible that you may have to do this again someday in the future, but in the meantime the problem disappears. **Note:** If the burn goes down to the carpet backing, or if you're unsure of all this, call a professional before you do anything. It's likely that he or she will have a brilliant (albeit more expensive) idea, like installing a patch or doing a carpet equivalent of a face-lift.

130. Dust Mites

I saw a picture of a dust mite, and it's freaking me out. These mites seem to be everywhere, according to the article I read. I don't want those ugly things in my house! What should I do?

The first thing I suggest is that you relax. Just because we are only now discovering dust mites doesn't mean that they are a new menace. They have probably been around since the dinosaurs. They were certainly present in your mother's and grandmother's homes, yet your family survived them intact.

How important they are to you really depends on whether anyone in your home is allergic to them. The allergen usually isn't so much the dust mite itself as dust mite "dust," composed mainly of assorted dust-mite body parts and feces. If nobody is allergic, there's nothing to be concerned about. Keep the little critters to a minimum with routine housecleaning, per-

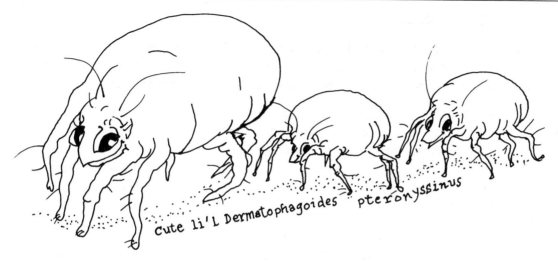

Cute li'L Dermatophagoides pteronyssinus

haps paying particular attention to laundering the bedding regularly as well as vacuuming mattresses and upholstered furniture with care. If you or family members do have allergies, advice from an allergist should be sought.

131. Mildew

Our family room is in the lower level of the house, below ground level. It smells musty down there, and now I've noticed brownish-black mildew stains in a couple of areas on my carpet. What should I do?

This is one of those problems that we probably can't solve, but we can at least help you avoid creating the same situation again in the future. Mildew in the carpet destroys the carpet and the backing by eating natural materials such as wool, jute, or cotton. What's left of these food sources are fibers with very little strength. When moved, the carpet may fall apart. Even if you leave it in place, the stains are nearly always permanent. Sorry. But here's what to do to prevent it from happening again:

1. When you replace the carpeting, select both a carpet and a carpet pad that are 100 percent synthetic. (Mildew eats only natural materials.)
2. Before installation, if the floor is concrete, make sure it is properly sealed. It probably isn't, and moisture seeping up through the concrete will encourage mildew growth. Consult a professional at a paint store for advice on a sealer.
3. If moisture is still a problem, install a dehumidifier.

Chapter 7

WINDOWS

132. Equipment

For years you've been telling us to forget silly hints about washing windows (like vinegar and newspapers, for example) and learn to clean them the way pros do. Old habits are hard to change, but I'm ready to learn—I hope! How do I start?

Congratulations! Soon you'll be cleaning like a pro, and we both can feel superior to all those out there sweating and swearing their way through what could—and should—be a much quicker and more satisfying job.

You won't get anywhere without a good *squeegee*—but not one of those lame ones you see in bargain bins for $1.19. The latter's lack of quality is one of the reasons squeegees have a bad reputation among consumers.

scrubber

There are three parts to a professional squeegee: (1) a handle (preferably one that swivels), (2) a replaceable rubber blade with a very smooth edge, and (3) an interchangeable rigid channel to support the blade.

As long as you can reach the tops of the windows, the only other thing you'll need is a bucket, some water with liquid dishwashing soap or a window-washing clear *ammonia solution,* and a few *cleaning cloths.* For out-of-reach windows, use an extension pole and a *window scrubber.* To determine how long the extension pole should be, measure the distance from the top of the windows to the ground and deduct your own height. A four-foot pole will suffice for most windows, while a fourteen-foot pole will reach most second-story windows. Use a window scrubber at the end of the extension pole to wash out-of-reach windows. Then replace the scrubber with the squeegee, and wipe the window clean and dry.

133. Extension Pole Etiquette

Using a squeegee is so much easier than my old way of washing windows. However, I'm having one problem with the extension pole. I have very tall and large windows. When I'm cleaning them, especially inside the house, that pole is downright dangerous.

I've had several accidents with a lamp and one each with my cat and my bird. No one has gotten hurt yet, but before someone or something does, what am I doing wrong?

Ooops. Sorry to hear that your enthusiasm for window washing has resulted in domestic mayhem. Do the cat and bird now get jittery whenever you reach for the pole?

The problem is that you're using the pole to clean windows within reach. The pole is relatively harmless when deployed vertically—i.e., on high windows or on the top portions of tall windows that are out of reach. When you lower the extension pole too far, thereby poking it behind you, it causes havoc among the pets and accessories in your house.

Here's what to do. Use the pole first with the *window scrubber* and then with the *squeegee* on the out-of-reach window areas. Then set the pole aside (keep it vertical!), and clean the lower part of the windows with just the squeegee. Use this same technique when washing the outside windows. Finally, why tempt fate? Take a look around, and evacuate vulnerable animate and inanimate objects before you start on the windows.

134.   Extension Poles

Should I get a second extension pole for my window scrubber?

No. It's more difficult to manage a second extension pole than it is to take the *squeegee* and *window scrubber* off and on as needed.

135.   Streaks

Screeeeeeeech! My windows are all streaky even though I used a squeegee. I'm ready to throw it out. It's all your fault, right?

starter strip

Now, now. If you're already using a *squeegee*, streaks probably mean that you have to make just a small adjustment in your technique. There are five secrets to avoiding streaks.

Secret Number One. Always start the squeegee on a dry area of the glass. After washing the window, create a dry "starter strip" for the squeegee either by wiping with a *cleaning cloth* or by using the end of the squeegee. If you stop the squeegee midway through a window, restart the subsequent strokes in the dry area.

Secret Number Two. Always use a dry squeegee. Wipe the blade dry with a cleaning cloth after every pass on the window.

Secret Number Three. Don't wash windows in the direct sun. The cleaning solution dries too quickly to avoid streaks.

Secret Number Four. Don't use any more soap or clear *ammonia* than is absolutely necessary. The more "product" you have in the water, the more likely it is that some of it will be left on the glass as a streak.

Secret Number Five. Make sure the squeegee blade is in good condition. A nick in the edge will leave a streak with each pull of the squeegee.

There. I hope you feel better. I certainly do.

136.　Furniture in the Way

I've read about how to clean windows using a squeegee. The illustration was a piece of glass with no frame, no curtains, no couch in front of it, no plants, and no end tables. You get the idea. I can barely get to my windows to open and close the curtains! I would rather have dirty windows than have to move everything necessary to be able to stand in front of them to clean them! Any other solution?

We don't blame you. You don't have to rearrange the furniture to be able to wash the windows. Use a *squeegee* with a pivoting handle along with an extension pole, if needed, so you can stand to the side of the window while cleaning it—perhaps the same place you stand to open and close the curtains. But it would be easier if there were a bit of a path. **Note:** There is

a fabulous little book by the name of *Clutter Control* (by yours truly [New York: Dell]) that can help point you in that direction.

137. French Panes

My house has many, many tiny windows—French panes. I don't use a squeegee on them, right?

As long as the panes are at least six inches in height *or* width, get a *squeegee* with a six-inch blade, and you'll be able to clean them faster than you ever thought possible. Wash several windows at a time, and then squeegee them. It's much faster than spraying them with glass cleaner and wiping each one dry.

138. Squeegee Exceptions

When cleaning windows, are there any situations in which using Blue Juice and cleaning cloths is better than using a squeegee?

I can think of only three "squeegeeless" situations: (1) when the window has uneven surfaces, such as a stained glass window; (2) when a large window has only a few fingerprints (or noseprints) but is otherwise clean; (3) when the window is smaller than the smallest *squeegee* blade.

139.   Hard-Water Spots

How do I get hard-water spots off windows?

If it's just a few small windows, *Tile Juice* or a similar acidic cleaner will work. Use it with a *white pad* or with #0000 steel wool. Tile Juice won't harm many surfaces, but rinse well to be on the safe side. If the stains are large or are on multiple windows, I recommend calling a professional. Special acid washes that remove hard-water stains from windows are available, but they're used generally by professionals. **Note:** Figure out what caused the stains, so they won't recur. The most common source is a sprinkler splashing water on the window. Adjust the sprinkler so it can't happen again.

140.   The Frames

I did a great job with my windows, but then my window frames and sills (all painted white) looked terrible—especially next to the nice clean windows. So I tried to clean the frames and got the windows dirty again in the process. How do you clean the frames without getting the windows dirty?

You don't. Clean the frames, including the sill, *first*—just before you clean the windows. Carry a *dusting brush, Red Juice,* and a *toothbrush* along with your window-cleaning equipment. Before you wash the window:

(1) use the dusting brush to remove dry dirt and cobwebs; (2) spray the frame and sill with Red Juice; (3) use the toothbrush to agitate in the corners and nooks and crannies; (4) wipe with a *cleaning cloth. Then* wash the windows immediately afterward. **Note:** Always plan on washing the frames when you set out to wash the windows. Also wash the area exposed when the window opens, plus any opening or closing mechanisms.

141.   Aluminum Frames

How do I clean aluminum window frames?

Use detergent and warm water. Even if the aluminum is pitted, be careful of using abrasives (steel wool, scouring powder, or green pads) because they will permanently scratch aluminum. Once aluminum is pitted, it's almost impossible to restore. If you would prefer the scratches to the corrosion, use a soap-filled steel wool pad. Rinse the frames well to remove bits of steel wool that will later rust.

Most contemporary aluminum windows are anodized or permanently protected with a coat of baked-on enamel paint. Don't use anything on anodized aluminum except detergent and water, *Red Juice* and water, or a moderate clear *ammonia solution*. **Note:** Auto wax or a silicone spray will help prevent aluminum corrosion and pitting. 3M makes a marine aluminum polish that may help in your case.

142. Screens

Forget windows! Mine are easy to clean. It's the screens that are caked with grunge. How do you clean them?

I vacuum mine for several years before I resort to wet-cleaning them. Use the brush attachment of your vacuum cleaner. Do one side first in an up-and-down direction and then in a side-to-side direction. Repeat on the second side.

When they need wet cleaning, don't just squirt them with a hose (which is scarcely better than doing nothing). This is definitely an outside job, though. Mix a solution of liquid dishwashing soap and water in a bucket in the same ratio you use to wash dishes. You'll also need a brush, either a *tile brush* or a *soft-bristle brush* on a pole so you can stand upright. Lay the screen flat on a hard surface, such as a deck or driveway. Use the brush to clean first one side and then the other, rinse, and allow the screen to air-dry. If you have an old piece of carpeting to put down first, you can wash both sides at the same time by laying the screen on the carpeting. Wet the carpet first, then as you scrub the top of the screen, the carpeting is rubbing against the bottom side and cleaning it also. This cuts your time in half. Before you replace the screens, remember to vacuum and clean where they were. Use *Red Juice*—and a *toothbrush*, if necessary. **Note:** Remove and put in storage all the screens from windows you never open. This improves your view and reduces the number of dirty screens in your future. **Covetous Note:** I once read that Jacqueline Kennedy Onassis had screens that were installed directly below the windows of her Nantucket home, right in the wall cavity. Only when the window was raised was the screen pulled up into view. That sounds like the perfect screen—expensive though they must have been. However, if you ever build a house and must make decisions about windows and screens, no matter how you must juggle your budget, get screens that can be installed and removed from inside the house. This will save an enormous amount of time and annoyance. It's simple enough to remove them one at a time, vacuum them, and then reinstall them. Even when you must take them outside to clean, it's still much easier to carry them through the house instead of fighting with the shrubs and ladders.

Chapter 8

PRODUCTS

143. Aprons

Do I really need a cleaning apron?

Absolutely. There's no better way to save time cleaning than to carry your cleaning supplies so you can eliminate housecleaning's biggest time waster, backtracking! Nothing else allows you to save as much time and effort cleaning. We've tried everything else, including all sorts of trays, buckets, and bags.

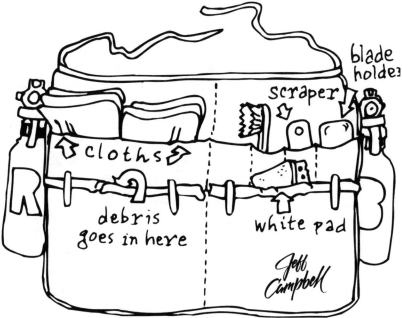

blade holder

scraper

cloths

debris goes in here

white pad

Jeff Campbell

144. Biodegradability

How can I tell if a cleaning product is biodegradable?

Essentially all liquid cleaners are biodegradable by loose definition. *Webster's* says only, "capable of being decomposed by natural biological processes." As we all know by now, it's the *length of time* that something takes to biodegrade that's important. In addition, new research at landfill sites shows that you must consider the circumstances in which an item will biodegrade. For example, some plastics may biodegrade within a few days in the direct sun but will essentially last forever if buried in a landfill. And don't forget, even a biodegradable cleaner may be packaged in an ecological disaster. In response to the public's rising concern for the environment, many manufacturers with a marketing department even half awake print a big, bold, colorful BIODEGRADABLE across their cleaner's label to appear to be as ecofriendly as possible. Whether these cleaners or their packaging are environmentally friendly is not at all clear. Until manufacturers are held to a stricter definition, a top priority for *The Clean Team* is to start with products that are "personally friendly"—that is, products that are safe and nonirritating to the human being using them. While sometimes similar, "environmentally" friendly and "personally" friendly are not always the same thing. But if you make sure you have products that are personally friendly around your home, you're well on your way to being environmentally friendly as well.

145. Concentrates

I was a little surprised at how much water I'm instructed to add to my concentrated liquid cleaner. It's practically all water. Is this okay? Or am I getting cheated?

No, you're not, but we think all that water is one reason concentrates have not been generally available until recently. Manufacturers were nervous it would lower our "perceived value" of their products. But the fact is most liquid cleaners are 90 percent or more water. That's okay. The important test is whether they work, not how much water they contain. Concentrates are a good idea. Besides saving money, they reduce packaging that ends up in our landfills, and they save trips to the store. Use them in good conscience. **Note:** Many people use more concentrate than the directions call for in the commonly held belief that if a little is good, then more is better. That's not true in this case. Using extra concentrate almost never improves effectiveness, but it does cause you to have to purchase the product again more quickly. Save the most money with concentrates by following the directions exactly.

146.   Are Disinfectants Necessary?

Is Red Juice a disinfectant? What about Simple Green, Fantastik, or similar all-purpose cleaners? After watching a recent TV ad, I feel guilty that I'm not being a good parent if I'm not using a disinfectant.

No, it's not. No, they're not. And you can be a wonderful parent and *not* use disinfectants. For regular housecleaning, disinfecting doesn't work the way you probably think it does. Even when a communicable disease is loose in your home, the items to disinfect are the shared things, such as the phone, eating utensils, and so forth, not every surface in the house. Here's why disinfecting isn't usually helpful in a household setting:

1. Germs (bacteria, viruses, fungi, et cetera) need warmth and moisture to survive. Simply wiping with soap and water removes many of them: The very act of cleaning results in a clean and dry surface hostile to their growth.
2. Even if a disinfectant is used, because a home is not a sterile environment, germs start growing again almost immediately.
3. Most disinfectants have to be left wet on a surface for ten minutes or so to be effective anyway.
4. Disinfectants work because they are poisonous—not only to bacteria and viruses but to larger living things, such as human beings. If you do

use them, take steps to protect yourself (e.g., avoid breathing fumes and wear rubber gloves). Here's what my friend Boston-area physician Geraldine Somers says on the subject: "In general, the health risks from many commonly used disinfectants hugely overbalance the almost imaginary risk from the organisms they are intended to kill." She adds, "As for toilet bowls, the bacteria in feces which cause disease have to be swallowed in order to cause infection—they don't jump out of the toilet bowl at us. (By the way, most organisms are species specific, so dogs are safe drinking toilet water—unless of course the water is full of toxic cleaners and disinfectants.)"

My viewpoint is simple: Keep the house clean and don't resort to routine use of disinfectants. Your home is not a hospital. That said, there is, as usual, another point of view. If you are one of those who believe you're really not adequately cleaning if you aren't slaughtering every last little bacterium as if you were Rambo himself, go right ahead. Two simple, effective, and inexpensive disinfectants are chlorine *bleach* and hydrogen peroxide—provided the surface will tolerate their bleaching effects. Geraldine reports that chlorine bleach kills bacteria, viruses (including HIV and hepatitis), fungi, and TB. Hydrogen peroxide (her favorite because it's the safest disinfectant around) kills bacteria, viruses, and fungi, but it doesn't kill TB. She also says that alcohol in 50 to 95 percent strength kills yeast, bacteria, many viruses, and TB, but it does not kill hepatitis B.

147.   Disinfecting Cleaning Brushes

What should I do to disinfect my toilet brush and my cleaning toothbrush before I put them back in my tray?

Rinse them in clean water, shake well, and allow them to air dry. As long as you allow them to dry thoroughly, many harmful microorganisms will perish. As an alternative, you can spray them with a disinfectant or *bleach solution.*

148.   More on Disinfection

I like the fact that you are so logical in your descriptions, pacing, et cetera. However, you don't ever mention disinfecting areas in the kitchen and bathroom. I have stopped using Red Juice in lieu of a commercial disinfectant (a Lysol product, Direct). Also I notice that you talk about "the toothbrush" used in the kitchen and the bathroom. Is this the same toothbrush for both jobs? If so, it isn't logical to carry a germ-laden toothbrush back into the kitchen. I don't think you address this in *Speed Cleaning*. Also, please remind your students that they should wash their hands be-

tween some of these jobs as well. I know that your book is read like a bible and followed to the T.

You're right that I don't talk much about disinfecting. As explained in Question 146, the process of cleaning disinfects well enough in the nonsterile environment found in our homes and is safer for the person doing the cleaning than is routine exposure to disinfectants. (Have you read the warning on a Lysol bottle lately?)

Having dedicated *toothbrushes* is a fine idea. Leave one under the sink in the kitchen and another in each bathroom so they are handy between weekly cleanings. Put another one in your carryall tray to use in other parts of the house. Regarding washing your hands: Many household bacteria can't cause illness unless they are swallowed. Washing your hands does help ensure that they won't accidentally make it into your mouth later on.

149. Dust Mops?

How do I know if I need a dust mop for home use?

If you have wood or other hard-surface floors in rooms besides the kitchen and bathrooms, and if you have one or more dust bunnies of any species, you do. (Kitchen and bathroom floors should be wet-mopped.) The floor attachment to a vacuum does a pretty good job of removing dust and debris from hard floors. But the vacuum doesn't "wipe" the surface of the floor the same way a dust mop does. Imagine vacuuming the top of a dusty glass table instead of wiping it with a cloth, and you will understand the difference between vacuuming and dust-mopping a floor. Also, a vacuum doesn't restore the floor's shine the way a dust mop does.

The best treatment for floors is a combination of both: vacuum the floors most of the time, and dust-mop only occasionally.

If your home has a rug over most of the hardwood, the hardwood is usually exposed for a foot or two around the edge of the rug. In such rooms a

dust mop isn't as effective as a vacuum. If you get a dust mop, though, make sure it is small enough to fit into that border without touching the carpet.

150. Double Duty as a Wet Mop

Can I use my dust mop as a wet mop?

I suppose so, but it's probably too dirty. Wetting a dust mop with cleaning solution and trying to wring it out by hand will prove to be a fiasco. It's better to dedicate it as a dust mop and use a *flat mop* or other good mop as a wet mop.

151. Washing Dust Mops

How and how often should I wash the dust mop head?

Don't wash it when it merely appears to be badly soiled, but rather when a good shaking doesn't get rid of loose debris or when you can't stand it any longer—whichever comes second. Wash it in warm or hot water in your washing machine. For best results, first put the dust-mop head into a *laundry net,* which keeps it from tangling and losing yarn during laundering. Bleach isn't recommended for dust mops, as it can weaken and shorten the life span of their fibers.

152.   Are Feather Dusters Effective?

I've tried feather dusters, but they just seem to stir up more dust than anything else. Do they really work? Am I doing something wrong, or do you have a particularly large supply of dusters you're trying to get rid of?

We really swear by feather dusters, but it's what we've learned along the way that allows us to be so cocky.

First, only 100-percent ostrich-down feathers reliably attract dust. Yes, ostriches have down feathers just as geese do. And just like the goose variety, ostrich down is softer, more pliable, and more valuable than run-of-the-mill feathers. Forget cheap synthetic dusters, brightly dyed chicken-feather dusters, or even regular ostrich feathers. They don't work. Ostrich down works, but it's not cheap. Expect to pay twenty-five dollars or so for a good ostrich-down duster. The length of the feathers isn't of primary importance; softness and flexibility are. Don't get too large a duster for normal households. Two-foot-long feathers are almost impossible to maneuver into tight spots without knocking over almost everything in sight.

To avoid stirring up dust it's essential to use the right dusting technique. Pull the feathers along the dusty surface, using a steady, even stroke. Come to a dead stop at the end of each stroke to avoid flinging dust into the air. When you lift the duster from the surface, the dust is attracted to the feathers by static electricity. Shake out accumulated dust from the feathers by tapping the duster against your ankle every once in a while. The dust then settles to the floor, where you can later vacuum it away.

By the way, feather dusters work well only when used to maintain a basically clean home. If your home (I mean other people's homes—not yours, of course) hasn't been dusted in six months, you (I mean they) must remove the accumulated dust with a vacuum or by wet-cleaning with a cloth. Then a feather duster can be employed on a regular basis.

Even if you have an ostrich-down duster and use it skillfully, you'll still have to polish and wipe occasionally. For example, you may be able to dust a seldom-used end table with a feather duster for weeks at a stretch, but eventually you'll have to reach for the furniture polish and a cloth to remove dust thoroughly and to enhance the surface shine. It's the same with baseboards. You can dust them most of the time with a feather duster, but they'll need an occasional swipe with *Red Juice* and a *cleaning cloth* to stay clean. And you would never use a feather duster on a dining table that's used three times a day. That table needs furniture polish and a *polishing cloth* or a good wiping each time you clean.

153. Wash Feathers?

Can a feather duster be washed?

Sure. They're just feathers, after all. (Lacking umbrellas, birds get wet all the time.) Wash them in the sink in a solution of warm water and dishwashing soap. Soak the duster for a few minutes, and then swish it around to loosen the accumulated dust and dirt. Repeat if necessary. Rinse thoroughly, squeeze excess water from the feathers, and allow it to air-dry with the feathers pointing down. Use a hair dryer if you can't wait to get back to dusting.

But don't think that just because you *can* wash it that you *must*. Clean it only if you've had an unfortunate experience, such as dropping it in dirty mop water or inadvertently dusting a muddy windowsill. **Note:** This method works equally well on your feather boa. Just do sections at a time.

154. MSDS (Material Safety Data Sheet)

What are MSDSs all about?

MSDS stands for "material safety data sheet." MSDSs are documents that detail what chemicals are contained in a product, what immediate and potential hazard(s) they may pose, precautions for handling and storing the

990 South Rogers Circle #5
Boca Raton, FL 33487-2848
For Information: 561-995-6900
For Emergencies: 1-800-255-3924

RED JUICE

Date Prepared
5-15-95

MATERIAL SAFETY DATA SHEET (MSDS)

Section 2 — Hazardous Ingredients/Identity Information

Hazardous Components (Specific Chemical Identity/Common Name(s))		OSHA PEL	ACGIH TLV	Other Limits	%(Optional)
Sodium Metasilicate	CAS#6834-92-0	2 mg/cubic mg	2 mg/cubic mg		

Section 3 — Physical/Chemical Characteristics

Boiling Point
212° F

Specific Gravity (H2O=1)
1.008

Vapor Pressure (mm Hg.)
Same as water

Melting Point
N/A

Vapor Density (AIR=1)
Same as water

Evaporation Rate (Water=1)
Same as water

Solubility in Water
N/D

Appearance and Odor
Thin light pink liquid, odorless

Section 4 — Fire and Explosion Hazard Data

Flash Point 1 (Method used)
None

Flammable Limits	LEL	UEL
N/A	N/A	N/A

Extinguishing Media
None

Special Fire Fighting Procedures
None

Unusual Fire and Explosion Hazards
None

Section 5 — Reactivity Data

Stability: Unstable	Stable	Conditions to avoid
	XX	N/A

Incompatibility (Materials to avoid)
Strong acids and oxidizers

Hazardous Decomposition or Byproducts
May produce oxides of carbon if incinerated

Hazardous Polymerization: May Occur	Will Not Occur	Conditions to Avoid
	XX	N/A

Continued on reverse

product, first aid in the event of exposure, what to do in an emergency, and so forth. Federal OSHA regulations require them to be available to anyone who asks. Their original purpose was to protect employees from short- or long-term negative health consequences from exposure to chemicals they might contact on the job. But interested consumers may request an MSDS for any cleaning product from the manufacturer or distributor. They are not standardized and can be somewhat difficult to decipher, but you'll find that they have important information (including emergency telephone numbers) if you take the time to study them.

155. Vacuum Amps

How many amps does a good vacuum cleaner have?

Contrary to what I was told by a devoted employee of a vacuum manufacturer, amps are not a good measure of a vacuum cleaner's performance. The amp rating tells you how strong the motor is, not necessarily how strong the suction power is.

Suction power is actually measured by "inches of water lift." Water lift measures, under test conditions, how high a vacuum can pull water up a tube. So my new and improved advice is to ask about the water-lift measurement of the vacuum. It should be listed in the vacuum's specifications. A good vacuum should be rated at seventy-five inches or more.

But your question brings me to one of my favorite pastimes, the Search for the Ideal Vacuum. *The Clean Team* has gone through quite a few vacuums since 1979, and we've tried every major brand. The ideal vacuum should:

- Be the canister type
- Have seventy-five inches (or more) water lift
- Be comfortable to hold and to use
- Have a long cord and a place to store the cord between uses
- Have an on/off switch that's easy to reach (preferably with your foot)
- Be able to vacuum under most furniture
- Not tip over when yanked by the hose
- Have a hose that *never* twists during use
- Have a handle for easy lifting
- Be light enough to make lifting less of a strain on your back
- Have a paper dust bag that's large enough to last for several weeks plus a pleated filter that traps particles down to 0.5 *micron*.

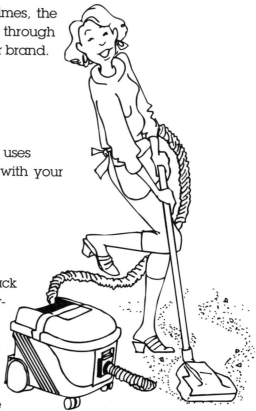

Of course I've never found the ideal vacuum. I don't believe one exists. This being the rather unfortunate case, get as many of these features as possible. The relative importance of the features depends on your own preferences. We've settled on a Swedish model we call the Big Vac.

On the basis of The Clean Team's experience I *wouldn't* purchase:

- A Kirby. It is too klunky, too heavy, too difficult to change bags, and has an array of attachments that will *never* get used.
- A Rainbow. The trouble to get the water in and out and the high price aren't compensated for by better performance. Its carpet and upholstery cleaner attachments are leaky and difficult to use.
- *Any* vacuum sold door to door. The reason it's so expensive isn't that it's better; it's that the salesperson earns a commission on each sale.
- *Any* vacuum that costs much more than four hundred dollars—or five hundred if very special special features (e.g., a *HEPA* filter) are included. We've paid fifteen hundred for a vacuum that works essentially the same as three-hundred-dollar models.

156.   Is a Beater Head Necessary?

I've read that you recommend a beater head for a vacuum, but I find it awkward. I like the other features of a canister vacuum, but much prefer using it *without* the beater head. I would feel better if I had your blessing.

Okay, you've got it. We used to recommend a beater head with a second motor because it "beats" the carpeting to loosen debris and because the beater brush sweeps pet hairs, string, lint, and other surface dirt up into the vacuum. However, vacuums have stronger suction now than they did when we first started using them almost twenty years ago. (They also have better filtration and other advances too.) With such improved suction, in many cases a beater head is *not* necessary. It all depends on what's in your home and what's being tracked into it. For example, the following situations have less of a demand for a beater head:

a well-designed floor attachment

1. The carpeting is low or medium pile.
2. You have area rugs on top of hard floors.
3. You have a front and a backyard.
4. You live in a condominium or apartment.
5. Your pets usually don't play in the dirt.

157. Vacuuming Pet Hair

Which vacuum does the best job of picking up dog and cat hair? I'm afraid I have it by the wheelbarrow full.

I know the feeling. It's truly amazing how much hair can come off even one dog or one cat. Most vacuums will pick up shed pet hair—as long as it's just lounging around on a hard-surface floor. The key factor is not so much the vacuum as the location of the hair. It's usually the fabric of the carpet or furniture or clothing that determines how difficult it will be to remove the hair. I realize that you often have no choice in such matters, but there is a window of opportunity when you purchase these goods. If you're a dog or cat person, consider pet-hair removal when you're shopping for new furniture. I've had great success with leather instead of fabric. Also consider color: don't get white carpeting if you have a black Lab.

When you can't change the carpet or furniture, the vacuum—and its attachments—become even more important. A canister vacuum with above-average suction—seventy-five inches or more of water lift—is recom-

mended. (See Question 155.) In addition, if you have plush carpeting or pets with long hair, a beater head is best for removing pet hair. Otherwise a well-designed floor attachment will remove hair satisfactorily. Besides getting under more furniture, a canister's hose separates to allow quick spot removal of pet hair or other debris as needed.

The most important attachment for removal of pet hair from upholstery is the one often called the furniture attachment. Look for one whose design uses soft rubber—either a solid piece of rubber or smaller "fingers" of rubber—to rub against pet hairs and pull them out of the furniture's fabric. Wash the rubber when it gets dirty to maintain its effectiveness.

If a vacuum isn't handy and there are a few pet hairs on furniture, spray your hand with a bit of *Blue Juice* or water and "wipe" the hairs with your hand. The hairs will gather together into a ball that can be easily picked up and discarded.

Probably the single most important thing you can do to combat pet hair is prevention. A neighbor of mine has two indoor cats, yet you will be hard pressed to find more than a couple of hairs in the entire apartment. The secret? The cats get a thorough brushing every day. I try to do the same with my two dogs—only outdoors. When I do, hair in the house is reduced by 90 percent or more. There are vacuum attachments designed to use directly on the animal. Many pets enjoy it—as long as they aren't frightened by the noise. **Note:** Limiting your pets to one sleeping spot can help concentrate the hairs and help with flea control at least in one area of the house . . . that is, until someone opens the front door and hair scatters everywhere.

Glossary

Acrylic Floor Finish

It's also referred to as "acrylic" and is often mistaken for a liquid wax. It is actually a type of liquid plastic floor finish. The purpose is the same, however: to add shine and provide protection for the floor. Examples are Future and the one we use, Clean Team High-Gloss Acrylic Floor Finish.

Ammonia, Clear

An old-fashioned cleaner that is hard to improve upon. It's best without the addition of suds, which just slow you down without increasing ammonia's effectiveness and also leave unwanted residues. Use ammonia for washing windows, mirrors, walls, ceilings, and floors. Use it in stronger ratios for very dirty floors, and all the way to full strength to remove heavy grease buildup and to strip wax or acrylic off floors (see *ammonia solution*). A glass saucer of full-strength ammonia left overnight in the oven is a safe oven cleaner. (At least it softens up the gunk.)

    If you don't enjoy the fumes, however, there are plenty of substitutes. Use

a mild solution of liquid dishwashing soap for windows. Use *Blue Juice* on mirrors and picture glass. Use *Red Juice* or trisodium phosphate on walls and ceilings. Use a general-purpose liquid cleaner (e.g., Sh-Clean, Armstrong, Mr. Clean, Pine Sol, et cetera) on floors. And use a specialized wax stripper (e.g., The Clean Team Acrylic Floor Stripper, Trewax, Instant Stripper, Bruce five-minute wax and acrylic remover) to remove wax or acrylic from floors.

Ammonia Solution

Don't worry about looking for a measuring cup when mixing ammonia. A dilute solution is a gurgle or so in a half bucket of water. Just keep adding more until it works well for the job at hand. It can be effective from extremely dilute to full strength. Use the following as guidelines only. Make your selection stronger or weaker as needed.

	Ratio	Approximate measurement
Window solution:	1:100	1 gurgle per gallon of water
Dilute solution:	1:20	3/4 cup per gallon of water
Moderate solution:	1:10	1 1/2 cups per gallon of water
Strong solution:	1:5 to full strength	3 cups per gallon of water

Apron, Cleaning

If you want to get the cleaning over with and move on to other things life has to offer, a cleaning apron is a must. It allows you to carry cleaning supplies with you and eliminate all that back-and-forth scurrying that wastes so much time. Carpenters don't run up and down a ladder every time they need another nail, do they? They wear tool belts to save time. Why not wear something similar while cleaning? Its pockets and loops allow you to keep everything you need at your fingertips as you work your way around a room—without having to backtrack. Avoiding this backtracking is the single most important step to reclaim your weekends. We suggest that you carry a standard kit of tools and supplies for routine cleaning. For some of the more specialized tasks described in this book, add the appropriate tool and/or cleaning agent for the duration of the task. (See page 207 for infor-

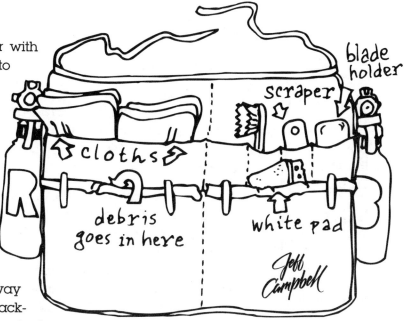

blade holder

scraper

cloths

debris goes in here

white pad

Jeff Campbell

mation on the apron or any other Clean Team product mentioned in this book.)

Bathroom Barrier

It provides an invisible, ultrathin, nonpermanent polymer coating that repels dirt, *soap scum,* and *hard-water spots.* Kind of like a wax coating on a car. Similar products are Rain-X and Glass Wax.

Bleach, Chlorine

A powerful, easily available, and inexpensive disinfectant, chlorine bleach is also a fast-acting assassin of mold and mildew on surfaces that can stand up to its color-removing properties. With respect to personal safety, however, it's obnoxious. It dissolves mucous membranes when inhaled, and it shouldn't be mixed with other household chemicals. Its environmental safety is debated. Industry spokespersons insist it does not harm the environment after it goes down the drain. Greenpeace adamantly disagrees—at least for industrial applications.

Bleach Solution

Consumer Reports recommends using bleach undiluted to kill mildew. According to Clorox, you may dilute it with twenty parts of water and it will still be effective against mildew. For serious mildew altercations, we use a solution of one part bleach to four parts water. For general disinfection and more cooperative mildew populations, 1:10 generally does the job. Clearly, you have the freedom to experiment a bit on your own, but err on the side of a weaker rather than stronger concentration, because bleach is an effective agent. Whatever dilution you settle on, let the bleach work for five to ten minutes and then rinse.

Blue Juice

The light-duty liquid cleaner used by *The Clean Team*. It is an industrial version of consumer products like Windex, Glass Plus, Formula 409 glass and surface cleaner, and so forth. Used mainly for cleaning glass: mirrors, picture glass, glass tables, et cetera.

Brushes

Brushes can increase the effectiveness of cleaning efforts many times over. They often last for years. Use them handheld on a pole, depending on the job to be done. Here are some brushes you'll find convenient to have around:

Dusting. It's really a good paintbrush, with natural bristles and feathered ends, but don't call it that or it'll disappear. Use it on wicker furniture, computer keyboards, lampshades, picture frames, molding, stereo equipment, light fixtures, the tops of books, car dashboards.

Stiff bristled. Same idea as a *toothbrush*, but for bigger jobs. Used to scrub grout lines between glazed and paver tiles, concrete floors, and patio stones. Also for scrubbing floors, greasy bricks, stove hoods, and many other rough surfaces. One aging former member of *The Clean Team* with arthritic knees and a touchy back swears by this brush: Attached to a long handle with a 360-degree swivel head, it can scrub surfaces without the operator having to bend over or kneel down.

Soft bristled. Use for wet-cleaning miniblinds, windows, and window screens.

Ceiling and wall. Use to remove spiderwebs and dust in high places.

Clean Team, The

Founded in 1979, The Clean Team Cleaning Service is San Francisco's busiest housecleaning service, cleaning over eighteen thousand times a year. We developed a method of cleaning now known as Speed Cleaning. Founded in 1987, The Clean Team Catalog Company offers cleaning products that are tested and selected by professional housecleaners to consumers via our mail-order catalog. Many of the products mentioned in this book and in our previous books are available through this catalog. (See p. 206.)

Cleaning Cloth

One hundred percent cotton cleaning cloths are more absorbent, are strong enough to allow real scrubbing, and can be used over and over again. They save cleaning time, and they save money compared with the cost of all the rolls of paper towels that you would otherwise purchase during their lifetime. Use white cloths only; dye can transfer to surfaces being cleaned.

Degreaser

An industrial-strength degreaser. For tough cleaning jobs including engines, oven hoods, bicycles, and power tools. Ours is called Monster Green. Look for the words *industrial strength* on other similar products.

De-Zov-All

A citrus-based *solvent* used to remove scuff marks, tar, grease, oil, gum, price-sticker residue, and so forth. Similar to De-Solv-It, Energine spot remover, Goo Gone, and other light-grade solvents, such as lighter fluid.

Dusting Brush See **Brush.**

Enzyme Cleaner

Enzymes are proteins created by living cells. When added to organic materials like grease, oil, blood, food, grass, pet accidents, vomit, et cetera, they immediately go to work breaking down the organic material within these substances. They are one of the most effective cleaning agents in reducing odors with organic origins. As long as you follow the directions, they are also harmless to you and your home. Our enzyme cleaner is called Stain Gobbler. (There are similar products offered specifically for pets. For example, ours is called Pet "OOPS" Remover.)

Eraser

Erasers are surprisingly good at removing black heel marks from floors. Also useful for removing spots, smoke, and smudges from hard surfaces. Close to being 100 percent safe for the user. No fumes, no toxic chemicals, no disposal problems, and they're downright cheap. Large gum erasers are the easiest to handle.

Fiberglass Cleaner

A nonabrasive cleaner formulated especially for fiberglass showers, tubs, boats, and so on. It is also good for cleaning marble, cultured marble, and acrylic spas and tubs. Gel-Coat is another example of this type of product.

Flat Mop

The European version of a mop that is greatly superior to the old-fashioned sponge or string variety and is infinitely better than any of the so-called miracle mops paraded endlessly on TV. It's basically a thick terry-cloth cotton towel wrapped around a large pad at the end of a swiveling handle. It covers more ground, is faster, and scrubs better than conventional mops. It gets into corners, even gets under most of the stove and refrigerator, and needs no bucket. Use it to wash walls and ceilings without the need of a ladder. When you're finished, you can toss its terry-cloth cover into the washing machine. It's like having a brand-new, sanitized, sparkling clean mop each time you use it. And for those of you who take no joy in wringing out a disgusting mophead, it's a godsend. It's the closest thing we've found to getting the superior results of traditional scrubbing with a cotton towel on hands and knees. It's simply the best mop we've found up to now.

Floor Coating

A long-lasting top coat applied (usually by applicator pad) to a floor. Polyurethane, Varathane, varnish, shellac, and paint are examples.

Floor Finish

A liquid or paste applied as a protective coat to a floor. *Acrylic* and liquid or paste wax are examples.

Floor Sealer

A liquid applied before the finish coat of *acrylic*. It contains solids called levelers that fill in microscopic imperfections in the floor finish. The result is a shinier-looking floor. Different versions are produced for wood floors, pavers, concrete, and more. They "seal" to protect against stains and moisture penetration and to add durability. Ours is named Floor Sealer; other examples are sold mostly at janitorial supply houses. Also see *grout sealer*.

Floor Wax

What our grandmothers used on their floors. The introduction of *acrylic floor finishes* and urethane *floor coatings* have pretty much made it extinct. Now when people talk about waxing a floor, they are generally referring to an acrylic floor finish. Fortified Floor Wax is our liquid version of old-fashioned paste wax. It is primarily used on varnish-coated floors. Other brand names include Johnson's paste wax and Trewax.

Furniture Feeder

The Clean Team's product for removing wax buildup from furniture. It is carnauba wax suspended in a *solvent*. The solvent removes grease and grime and previous coats of wax and replaces it with a new coat of carnauba wax. It also removes many coffee-cup and other types of furniture rings. Another effective brand is Howard Restor-A-Finish.

Grout Coloring Agent

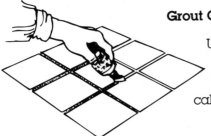

Used to cover up permanent stains in grout lines. Not a cleaner, it's more like a coat of paint over dirty grout. It cannot replace missing grout, no matter how hard you try. Our product is called Grout Whitener.

Grout Sealer

A product used to fill the pores and microscopic cracks in grout so they won't collect dirt or stains instead. Sealer should be applied on all newly installed grout. Reapply it per the manufacturer's instructions, generally once or twice a year. Besides grout, many finely pitted surfaces benefit from a sealer. Stone, brick, cement, crazed (finely cracked) tile, and other nonglazed tiles are examples. Our product is called Grout Sealer.

Hard-Water Spots (AKA Mineral Deposits, Lime, Scale, #*@!*#!)

These are the dissolved minerals left when hard water dries—calcium carbonate and magnesium, in most cases. An acidic cleaner (e.g., *Tile Juice* or Shower Power) plus a *white pad* or #0000 steel wool (or dynamite) is the weapon of choice.

HEPA

High-efficiency particulate air filter (often in three stages). A "true" HEPA filter will capture 99.97 percent of particles larger than 0.3 *micron*. But read the product's specs carefully: *HEPA* is a term applied somewhat overzealously these days. HEPA filters were originally developed to trap radioactive dust in atomic plants.

Inconspicuous Spot: Carpets

This is the legendary spot everyone says to try out a cleaner on, the Holy Grail of cleaning. The idea is that if the cleaner is going to devastate the area, it might as well be in this allegedly invisible zone. Have you ever wondered what you would do if you actually found it? If your target is a carpet, here's what folks at the Michigan State University Extension say to do. We're impressed enough to quote them in full, with their kind permission:

> To test a product, mix it according to directions or as it is planned to be used. In an inconspicuous area, such as in a corner, behind a chair, in back of the drapery, et cetera, place approximately one teaspoon of the solution on a spot about the size of a nickel. Work the solution in with the fingers, press a white tissue against the wet spot, and hold it there for about ten seconds. Examine the tissue to see if any dye has transferred. The amount transferred may be very small and difficult to see on the tissue, but over a large area of carpet it could be objectionable. If the small spot tested does not include all the different colors, then the others should be tested. Retest any color that may be in doubt. The wet spots should be carefully examined, as they may show a change not apparent on the tissues.
>
> This testing should show any damage or change that may take place on the fibers. The chance of damage occurring with a cleaning solution is very

small, but some spot-removal chemicals can damage some fibers. The fibers may become sticky, soft, or dissolve. Always test and examine carefully to prevent being sorry later.

If, during testing, a dye transfers or it appears as though a fiber is being damaged, then this product should not be used. Try testing other products until a safe one is found. If none can be safely used, then contact and explain the problem to a professional.

A second test will determine the type of residue that remains after the carpet or rug has been cleaned. The cleaning solution is made up of various chemicals and liquids. After this is applied, the liquid will start to evaporate. The drying time will vary from several hours to several days.

After the liquid evaporates, what type of material remains on the fibers? If it is a powdery, granular material, it will be removed with the vacuum. Any other consistency will remain on the face fibers.

To determine the type of residue, pour one-half cup of the product as it is to be used into a glass pie plate. Allow the pie plate to sit undisturbed until all the liquid has evaporated. This may take several days. The process can be speeded up by placing the pie plate, with the solution, in an oven at 160°F. Watch and remove the plate when no more liquid is being evaporated.

Examine the residue that remains. Is it sticky? If so, it will hold on to soil at an accelerated rate and make the carpet soil faster. The sticky residue will also hold the fibers together and the surface of the carpet will be more matted and less resilient. A hard, waxy residue will not hold on to soil to the same extent, but it will dull the surface and the fibers will not appear bright and clean.

Once the sticky or waxy residue gets on the fibers, it usually remains until the residue is flushed out with a lot of warm water. Another cleaning with the same solution will only build up the residue. If it is suspected that a residue is already present on the carpet yarns, place a tablespoon of warm water on a spot and work it in with the fingers. A foam or a slippery feeling will indicate a detergent residue. The best way to remove it is by the hot-water extraction method. Many professional rug cleaners have this type of equipment or it can be rented.

Just for fun, let's assume that you're not going to stop to perform these tests when someone has spilled red wine on your new white carpet before your very eyes. Instead you will proceed with great haste to blot up the wine and clean up any residual stain (see Question 119). However, if a stain has set (dried) on a carpet or upholstery, and you're going to try a stain-removing product (e.g., Carbona, Energine, Goo Gone, and K2r), perform at least the first part of the Michigan tests. Make sure, before you try to remove the stain, that the cleaning agent is not going to change the color of the carpet or upholstery. Even if it removes the stain, almost any change in color is worse because it is automatically going to loom larger than the original stain. Plus, it's *always* irreversible when you alter the color (you're bleaching it). The first Michigan test will also show you if the material's fibers are being damaged. If you're patient—or if you've learned by prior discouraging experience—complete all the Michigan tests. Think of how soundly you'll sleep that night!

Inconspicuous Spot: Flooring

By "flooring" we mean vinyl, polyurethane, tile, masonry, wood, and most other noncarpeted floor coverings. Once again, your first job is to find the test spot: in a closet, behind a door that's normally open, under a table or chair, and so on. As above, you don't have to pretest if you're wiping up a wet spill and using *Red Juice*. But you should pretest if you are planning to strip and rewax a floor, or if you are trying a stain-removing product on a set stain.

To test a stripper, mix up a bit of the product and, in that inconspicuous place, remove an area of wax (as small an area as you can manage, say one foot by one foot or so). Perform all the necessary stripping steps, including letting the floor dry, before you proceed. If you're planning to rewax, go ahead and apply wax to the stripped area. Apply as many coats as you plan to put on the floor, and allow each coat to dry before proceeding. Try to be sure—before you start sloshing strippers and wax all over the place—that you're going to be thrilled with the final result. If not, it's much more gratifying to quit now rather than at the end of a long day of hard and ultimately futile work!

Laundry Net

Holds washable items together in the washing machine so they can take proper advantage of all the agitation without tangling or shedding excessively. Good for washing dust-mop heads, aprons, and other items with ties, as well as delicate items.

Marble Polish

Ours is a liquid called Premium Marble Polish. Others include Goddards marble polish and Johnson's paste wax.

Micron

The unit of measurement sometimes used to describe what will pass through a filter such as a vacuum dust bag or an air purifier. One micron equals 1/25,000th of an inch (about the size of one bacterium or dust mite egg). Here are the approximate sizes of some of the smaller things inhabiting your home, in case you were wondering:

Sand	80 to 175 microns
Dust mites	100 to 150 microns
Human hair	30 to 120 microns
Pollen	20 to 100 microns
Threshold of visibility	10 microns
Fumes	2 to 8 microns
Dust mite eggs	0.3 to 1.5 microns
Dust mite feces	0.3 to 1.5 microns

Mop See **Flat Mop.**

Pet "OOPS" Remover See **Enzyme Cleaner.**

Polishing Cloth

Used to dust or to apply furniture polish. Softer than a cleaning cloth. We use disposable ones that are 100 percent cotton flannel and untreated with chemicals designed to make them attract dust. Even though they are disposable, they last for months.

Pro-Scrub

An even softer than Soft Scrub liquid cleanser. Besides Soft Scrub, there's Comet liquid gel and Dow smart cleanser with bleach.

Pumice Stick

Pumice cut into small blocks that are used to rub or abrade things like *hard-water spots* from a hard surface. Pumice sticks are dangerous to many surfaces but work well (when it may seem that nothing else does) on porcelain and other hard surfaces like tile. It's the same product used to clean swimming pools and to remove calluses.

Rabbit Ear Duster

An extension duster that can be bent to mimic the shape or angle of the surface to be dusted.

Red Juice

The heavy-duty liquid cleaner used by The Clean Team. It is an industrial version of consumer products like Fantastik, Mr. Clean, Pine Sol, Simple

Green, and Formula 409. As with our other favorites, Red Juice is by far the best one of this category we've ever found. It's nontoxic, odorless, biodegradable, and consistently excellent. Used to remove fingerprints, grease, and smudges of all kinds from countertops, walls, woodwork, shelves, cupboards, appliances, and many other surfaces. Also used to remove grease- and water-based stains from carpets and upholstery and to pretreat laundry.

Rust Remover

A cleanser with oxalic acid, which is an extremely powerful rust-removing agent. Ours is called Rust Remover. Other brand names include Bar Keepers Friend and Zud.

Scraper

Carried in a cleaning apron to be at your fingertips for removing mystery globs on counters, floors, or other durable hard surfaces. Otherwise known as a putty knife. The new plastic ones are safer on more surfaces and so have greater utility, if not greater longevity.

Sealer See **Floor Sealer** and **Grout Sealer.**

Soap Scum

The fatty residue of soap that clings to mineral deposits and many other surfaces, including glass and probably people. It's relatively easy to remove.
Dissolve the scum with a bathroom cleaner, such as *Pro-Scrub* or powdered
cleanser, such as Comet, wipe and/or agitate with a *tile brush*, and rinse
away. Often mistaken for *hard-water spots*.

Soft-Bristled Brush See **Brush.**

Stiff-Bristled Floor Brush See **Brush.**

Solvents

Water is known as the universal solvent, but most of us think of solvents
such as dry-cleaning fluid, mineral spirits, turpentine, and the like when the
subject is cleaning.

The solvents we're talking about here work on oil-based, not water-
based, stains. Water-based stains are usually cleaned with products like
ammonia, *Red Juice*, and *Blue Juice*. Accordingly, it's best not to apply an
oil-based solvent if the surface is wet with water. It can cause a gooey mess
and a ring.

In approximate order of increasing strength and therefore of both nice and nasty consequences, here are the solvents that are likely to be used in household cleaning:

Solvent	Applications
Lighter fluid Kerosene Paint thinner De-Zov-All Citrus-based solvents Endust WD-40	Gummy label residue from hell, stuck-on tape, crayon and heel marks, chewing gum, grease, oil, tar, wax, and anything that vaguely resembles an oil-based product or goo in general. Lighter fluid is our all-around favorite. (Slips nicely into a cleaning apron too.)
Alcohol	Useful mainly to speed up the evaporation of products like glass cleaners. It can dull many plastics. It's great for removing hair spray from mirrors and similar hard surfaces.
Nail-polish remover Cleaning fluid (e.g., Carbona) Acetone Lacquer thinner	These solvents will take care of anything their milder cousins can—and then some. Provided your carpet doesn't melt, lacquer thinner will remove almost any oil-based product. Apply to the spot, agitate with a *toothbrush* briefly, then blot up with a *cleaning cloth,* using a twisting motion. And just because a solvent like nail-polish remover may smell okay to some people, it doesn't mean that it isn't terrorizing your liver.

Don't use any of these solvents without pretesting in that mythical *inconspicuous spot*. They are adept at dissolving dirt, but they don't know the difference between dirt and the surface underneath. Lighter fluid—the lightest of the listed solvents—is safe for a huge range of surfaces, but even it can damage certain soft plastics and rubber. Lacquer thinner is a champion solvent for difficult oil-based stains on many carpets—and it leaves no residue—but it is strong enough to eat right through the bottom of a plastic cup. Kindly note that lacquer thinner has a skull and crossbones on its label. In addition, all these solvents are flammable, so don't wave a lit cigarette in their direction. Neither should you feed them to anyone or anything, or splash them in your eyes, or inhale their fumes in a poorly ventilated area. So use solvents only if more sensible methods won't work.

rubber blade

blade channel

swivel handle

Squeegee

There are two kinds. One (metal) is the only realistic choice for washing windows. The other (plastic) keeps hard water from becoming a big problem on shower doors and walls.

Tile Brush

This brush started out cleaning large milk containers in commercial dairies. Then it saw demand in the auto industry as a dandy automotive wheel-cleaning brush. *The Clean Team* discovered that it's also great for digging into the *soap scum* and *hard-water spots* that build up on tile and grout. Its design allows you to reach into nasty corners, grout lines, and other obnoxious hard-to-reach places.

Tile Juice

The Clean Team's choice over things like Lime-A-Way, Dow bathroom cleaner, X-14, Shower Power, Lysol basin, tub, and tile cleaner, and so forth for removing *hard-water spots*, *soap scum*, and heavy accumulation of plain old dirt from tubs and showers.

Toilet Brush

For even this simple household item we have strong opinions about what works and what doesn't work. The best ones—which luckily enough are often the least expensive—are all plastic (no twisted wire), have stiff bristles for good scrubbing action, are shaped to reach deep into the toilet neck and under the toilet rim, and have a handle long enough to keep the user satisfyingly distant.

Toothbrush

It looks like a dental toothbrush, but it's really a serious cleaning tool that can clean practically anything *but* teeth. It has strong bristles and a shape that allows you to scrub without banging your knuckles in the process.

Vinegar, White

White vinegar is 5 percent acetic acid—the mildest acid available. Sometimes suggested as a floor cleaner or as a safer alternative cleaner for removing *hard-water spots* in the shower. It's not particularly effective for either of these jobs because it's so mild. This mildness can be overcome when something with hard-water deposits can be soaked in it. Examples are shower heads or deposits in vases. It's acidic, so don't use it on marble. It can also be used in a dishwasher to remove stains.

Wet/Dry Vacuum Cleaner

It's great for removing water and cleaning solutions when washing floors. Useful in emergencies to remove most liquids after an accident (e.g., spilled wine on a carpet). Also handy for cleaning out indoor or outdoor fountains and the filter housing for a swimming pool.

White Scrub Pad (White Pad)

A modern abrasive material, usually a sponge on one side and a white pad on the other. Use when a *cleaning cloth* or *toothbrush* aren't strong enough. It's far less likely to scratch a surface than any other color pad (e.g., green, black, et cetera), yet it's almost as effective for most household uses. Use wet, and make sure you're not pressing so hard that you're scratching the surface. Also offered by 3M (Scotch-Brite), O-Cel-O, and S.O.S.

Window Scrubber

A brush used, along with a *squeegee*, to clean windows. Essential—along with an extension pole—for windows that are out of reach.

Appendix

HOW TO ORDER TOOLS, EQUIPMENT, AND SUPPLIES

It makes little sense to us to write about cleaning solutions if we don't offer some way of enabling you to find the products we mentioned.

Because we use cleaning products daily and test new ones regularly, we have developed very definite opinions about them. We know what works and won't tolerate anything that doesn't. Some of the products have higher initial costs, but they last two or three times longer than the cheaper alternatives. Others have replaceable parts that save money in the long run. And others cost more but just plain work better. For example, even if those cheap chicken-feather dusters you see in the grocery stores were free, we still wouldn't use them because they don't work. We much prefer to use ostrich-down feather dusters that work and that save time week after week. And if something new comes along that works better, we change products. We aren't committed to any brand name or manufacturer—only to excellence.

One way to save time in your own housecleaning is to skip all the tests and trials of products that we do. But even if you know what products you want to use, it still takes time to purchase them—especially if they're not carried at the local grocery or hardware store, as is true of many of the professional products we use. Our catalog can save you time on both accounts, because you can make your choices without leaving your home. The only products we offer are the best ones we've found so far—and we're still looking after all these years.

If you would like a free copy of our catalog, please write us at:

The Clean Team
990 S. Rogers Circle, #5
Boca Raton, FL 33487

If you're in a hurry, call us at **1-800-717-CLEAN**, and we'll mail you one the same day. Or call us anytime for solutions to your toughest cleaning questions.

Or visit our Web site at:

http://www.JeffCampbell.com

Index

(Numbers refer to page numbers, not question numbers.)

Acids: 17, 28, 50, 71, 111, 122
   cleaners: 41, 50
   oxalic: 19, 54
Acrylic
   floor finish: 179
   tubs: 47
Adhesives: 30, 46, 139, 186
Ammonia
   clear: 179
   solution: 180
Appliances, small: 32
Apron, cleaning: 159, 181
Artwork: 68

Baby formula: 79
Backsplashes: 21
Bathroom Barrier: 182
Biodegradability: 160
Bleach, chlorine: 14, 55, 82, 141, 163, 182
   solution: 183
Blinds, wood: 101

Blood: 134
Blue Juice: 6, 183
Body odor: 91
Brass
   bathroom: 45
   discoloration: 63
   film: 65
   lacquered: 63
   sconces: 65
Brick
   fireplaces: 77
   greasy: 22
Brushes: 183–184, 203–205
Burned spots: 143
Butcher block: 12

Cabinets, wood: 10
Can openers: 32
Candle wax: 71
Carpets
   mildew: 146
   stains: 128

   traffic areas: 132
Ceramics: 67
Chandeliers: 92
Chrome: 41
Cleaning alone: 58
Cleaning cloths: 185
Cleaning questions hotline: 9
Cloths
   cleaning: 185
   polishing: 197
Cobwebs: 85
Corian: 50
Countertops: 13
   Corian: 50
   grouted: 35
Crayon marks: 73
Cribs: 79

Degreaser: 186
Desk, rolltop: 91
De-Zov-All: 186
Dishwasher: 31

odoriferous: 27
Disinfection: 162, 164
  brushes: 164
  toilets: 56
Doors, accordion: 80
Dust mites: 144
Dust mops: 165–167
  rabbit-ear: 198
Dusting: 61–62, 66, 83, 168

Enzymes: 55, 81, 136, 186
Eraser: 187

Fans, ceiling: 94
Feather dusters: 168, 170
Feces: 137
Fiberglass
  cleaner: 187
  showers: 40, 41
Filter, stove hood: 20
Fingerprints: 78
Fireplace, brick: 77
Fleas: 88
Floors
  Armstrong: 111, 120
  coatings: 103, 109, 189
  concrete: 125
  finishes: 103, 109, 189
  heavy traffic: 104, 118
  linoleum: 50
  maintaining: 118, 125

marble: 122–123
Mop & Glo: 120
mopping: 121
no-wax, stripping: 116
  waxing: 115
polyurethane: 104–105, 108
protection: 126
sealing: 119, 189
skid marks: 112
stripping: 109
varnish: 106
and vinegar: 111
vinyl: 111, 114
  stripping: 115
water stains: 110
wax: 190
waxing: 117
wood
  care: 106
  cleaning: 107–108
  stripping: 109
Frog, bikini-clad: 67
Furniture
  Feeder: 190
  upholstery, body odor: 91
  wax: 69
  wicker: 90

Granite: 15
Grease
  degreaser: 186

on backsplashes: 21
on bricks: 22
on cabinets: 10
on carpets: 138
on grout: 35
on stove exhausts: 20
on stovetops: 25
Grout
  color: 36–37, 190
  countertop: 35
  film: 37
  floor: 36
  mildew: 37
  regrouting: 35
  sealer: 35, 37, 191
  shower: 35, 41
  urine upon: 55
Gum: 139

Hair spray: 52
Hard-water spots: 28, 30–31, 40–45, 49,
  54, 66, 155, 191
Heel marks, black: 113
Help! 9
HEPA filters: 191
Hinges, cabinet: 11
Hydrogen peroxide: 15, 55, 163

Inconspicuous spot, legendary: 192

Juice, Blue: 6, 183
Juice, Red: 6, 198

Knickknacks: 67, 84

Lamp shades: 66
Laundry net: 196
Levolors: 96, 100
Lime deposits: 28, 30–31, 40–45, 49, 54,
    66, 155, 191

Marble
    bar: 70
    cleaning: 17
    cultured: 50
    floors: 122–123
    polishing: 122–123, 196
Material Safety Data Sheets: 170
Micron: 196
Mildew
    carpets: 146
    closet: 81
    grout: 37
    prevention: 38, 82
    shower: 40
Mineral deposits: 28, 30–31, 40–45, 49,
    54, 66, 155, 191
Miniblinds: 96, 100
"Miracle" mops: 23
Mirrors, streaked: 42

Mites, dust: 144
Mop & Glo: 120
Mopping: 121
Mops: 23, 165–166, 188
MSDSs: 170

Net, laundry: 196
Nicotine: 75
Nonslip strips: 46, 50

Openers, can: 32
Ovens
    self-cleaning: 24
    conventional:
Oxalic acid: 19, 54–55, 199

Paint: 76, 78, 87
Paintings, fine art: 68
Paver tile: 124
Peroxide, hydrogen: 15, 55, 163
Pets
    feces: 137
    hair: 175
    urine: 135
Pigs, rampaging: 87
Plants
    dried: 62
    silk: 61
Polish
    marble: 196

shoe: 133
Posters, wall: 75
Poultices: 16, 110
Pro-Scrub: 198
Pumice stick: 53, 198

Question hotline: 9

Rabbit-ear duster: 198
Radiators: 79
Red Juice: 6, 198
Rings
    furniture: 60
    toilet: 52
    white: 60
Rust
    Remover: 199
    stainless steel sink: 19
    toilet bowl: 54

Safety: 8, 12, 108, 112, 170, 182
Salmonella: 12
Salt and pepper shakers: 32
Scale: 28, 30–31, 40–45, 49, 54, 66, 155,
    191
Sconces: 65
Scraper: 199
Scrub pad, white: 205
Scuff marks: 113
Scum, soap: 40–41, 45, 49, 200

Sealer, grout: 36–37
Shades, lamp: 66
Shoe polish: 133
Showers
    curtains: 48
    doors: 42–43
    heads: 43
    liners: 49
    walls: 43
Sinks
    porcelain: 17
    stainless steel: 19
Skid marks: 112
Soap scum: 40–41, 45, 49, 200
Solvents: 41, 47, 200
Soot: 76
Spot, inconspicuous, legendary: 192
Squeegees: 42–43, 147, 152, 154, 202
Stainless steel
    sinks: 19
    stove hoods: 20
Stains
    blood: 134
    carpet: 128
    countertop: 13
    dishwasher: 28
    oil: 17
    permanent: 50
    porcelain: 17
    red wine: 129

shoe polish: 133
stove top: 27
tea: 15
toilet bowl: 52
tough: 41
water: 110
Stickers: 30
Stone: 17
Stoves
    burners: 25, 26
    exhaust filter: 20
    exhaust hood: 20
    glass-top: 26
Streaks
    glass: 151
    mirror: 42
Strips, nonslip: 46, 50

Tape residue: 139
Tea stains: 15
Teenagers: 56
Terra cotta: 31, 110, 124
Tile
    backsplash: 21
    bathroom: 45
    Juice: 203
    pavers: 124, 189
Toilet
    brush: 203
    disinfecting: 56

rings: 52
seats, oak: 55
stains: 54
Toothbrush: 204
Tubs
    acrylic: 47
    resurfaced: 49

Upholstery: 91
Urine
    on grout: 55
    pet: 135

Vacuuming: 125, 175
Vacuums: 173–174
    amps: 172
    wet/dry: 36, 131, 205
Vase, glass: 66
Vinegar, white: 204

Wallpaper: 65
    crayons: 73
    and grease: 74
Water, hard/soft: 44
Wax
    buildup: 69
    candle: 71
White scrub pad: 205
Wicker: 90

Windows: 151
    aluminum frames: 156
    and Blue Juice: 154
    extension poles: 148, 151
    frames: 155

French panes: 154
high: 148–149, 150–151
hard-water spots: 155
screens: 157
scrubber: 205

squeegees: 147, 152, 154
streaks: 151
Wine, red, spills: 129
Working alone: 58